atd
PRESS

TORY

TRAINING

Selecting and Shaping Stories

That Connect

HADIYA NURIDDIN

ATD Press is an internationally renowned source of insightful and practical information
on talent development, training, and professional development.

ATD Press
1640 King Street
Alexandria, VA 22314 USA

Ordering information: Books published by ATD Press can be purchased by visiting ATD's
website at www.td.org/books or by calling 800.628.2783 or 703.683.8100.

Library of Congress Control Number: 2018930647

ISBN-10: 1-56286-689-3
ISBN-13: 978-1-56286-689-1
e-ISBN: 978-1-56286-690-7

ATD Press Editorial Staff
Director: Kristine Luecker
Manager: Melissa Jones
Community of Practice Manager, Learning & Development: Amanda Smith
Developmental Editor: Kathryn Stafford
Text Design: Jason Mann
Cover Design: Tim Green, Faceout Studio

Printed by Color House Graphics, Grand Rapids, MI

To my mother, Badriyyah Nuriddin, for her love, dedication, and friendship

To my father, Asmar Nuriddin, for his love, encouragement, and support

To my sister, Alex Morris, for showing me what strength looks like

Contents

Finding the Storyteller

t was a training emergency. Human resources at the bank where I had been working for about three years had just reversed the annual performance management scale so that the best performers, who were previously given "1" ratings, would now receive "5" ratings. The bank's performance management course now had to be updated to reflect the change. My manager asked me to take the lead and then teach the course a few weeks later.

It was the early 2000s and instructional design was new to me, but as I worked through the course, it soon became clear that it was not a course at all. It was human resources policies copied onto slides. I shuddered at the thought of spending two days reading sections of the employee handbook aloud to a group. The course needed to be redesigned, but at that point in my career, I had only designed and facilitated courses that were a few hours long—never a multiday class like this one. I agreed to teach the current course, but asked my manager to let me design a brand-new performance management course to teach the next time around. He agreed.

I used the case study approach and created characters whom the participants would take through the performance management process. It had a lot of moving parts and was unlike any of the other management courses our training department offered. My course design was probably needlessly complicated, but I wanted to add variability, and that was difficult to do with only static worksheets and participant guides.

After a month of designing, writing, and getting feedback from other trainers, it was time to teach my new two-day course. I was nervous— scared that I would forget to copy a worksheet or a game card or some other component that the participants would need. I invested so much time and energy into this course because it marked the beginning of my transition from trainer to serious instructional designer. I obsessed over everything that could go wrong. How would I remember everything? What if the course ran too long or too short? Would people like it?

On the first day, at 8:35 a.m., I started with a scenario to get the participants engaged. I then asked them to introduce themselves. Half way through the introductions, it became apparent that I had the least amount of work experience in the room. I stopped asking follow-up questions and just stared as each person talked about how many people they managed and how long they had been in their current leadership role. When introductions were finished, I felt numb as I faced 20 people who had each spent a minimum of five years in management. Most had been managers longer than I had been an adult.

For the first time, throughout the design and delivery process of the course, I came face-to-face with the reality that I had never been a manager in my life. I had never managed anyone's performance, so I had never given a performance review. I had never talked to anyone about giving a performance review. I had zero experience assessing performance, coaching, or giving feedback. All I knew was the content I was given as source material for the course, and my own experience receiving performance reviews. And while I had taught many classes on topics I had no experience in before, this felt different because instead of teaching them how to do something new, I was coaching them on how to improve a job they had been doing for years—a job I'd never had. I was in way over my head.

How Do You Solve a Problem Like Darla?

I was able to get through that first morning by focusing on the content. I avoided being exposed as the fraud that I felt like I was until we started discussing the case studies. There were four, each one assigned to a group of five participants. Each study featured a different character who had one of four core traits: ambitious, lazy, mediocre, or combative. My combative character, Darla, also used to be each participant's fictional peer. She received the most attention—as is often the case with problem employees. The case study had details about each employee's imaginary work and personal life, but the group assigned to Darla took the liberty of giving her a backstory they made up based on their experiences with problem employees. They vilified Darla in ways I could have never dreamed up.

It turned out that employees like Darla were the reason everyone was there. They could manage good employees—or so they thought—but people like Darla had driven them to take the course. Most wanted to fire Darla immediately after reading one of her sarcastic emails. When I told them that they had no grounds to fire her, they naturally wanted to know what they were supposed to do. Could they transfer her to another branch? Should they begin progressive discipline? Should they just ignore her? They did not want to hear more theories. They did not want to hear what other participants had tried. They wanted to hear what they were supposed to do about a problem like Darla from me, a trainer in the human resources department and, obviously, an experienced manager (or why else would I be teaching the course?). I, of all people, must know.

I did not.

During lunch, I considered my options. I felt my credibility slipping, and I needed to do something about it. I concluded that the group was not asking me how to deal with Darla, but how to avoid dealing with her. Making a problem disappear was easier than taking it head-on. But I knew that just telling them that would not work—they were beyond that point. I also noticed my attitude toward the group changing. I wanted to defend this made-up woman who had aroused so many emotions. I was bothered by how they talked about her and I wanted to suggest that they try empathy. While it was not the answer they were looking for, empathy is always a step in the right direction.

"Why Don't You Like Me?"

After welcoming everyone back from lunch, still unsure of what to do, I decided to say what was on my mind:

> About a year or two after graduating from college, I worked in a copy shop. I was not a manager or a supervisor. I made the actual copies. This was not the good fortune my bachelor's degree was supposed to bring me, but it's where I was, and I was not happy about it. I did my job, but I had a manager and hated it. I didn't hate my manager specifically. I hated that I had a manager. I undermined him behind his back by giving my co-workers unsolicited opinions on everything from the way he managed our last meeting to what kind of car he drove.
>
> After a few months of this, he confronted me during a performance review.
>
> "Why don't you like me?" he asked.
>
> "What?" I replied, holding my hand to my chest to cover the wound. I was shocked.
>
> "I know you don't like me," he said, his voice trembling a bit, but never looking away. "That's fine. I'm not everyone's cup of tea, but people do like and respect you, and your opinion matters to them."
>
> I was putting together a defense in my head, but all that came out was a deflated, "But. . . ."
>
> "All I ask is that if you have a problem with me, come to me," he continued. "Don't tell everyone how you feel. It's not fair to them because they don't have enough information to form their own opinions. Deal?"
>
> I stared at him. I could tell he was tired of far more than just me. Perhaps he didn't think he should be there either and he wanted more, too. Whatever that "more" was, perhaps

fighting so much for so little reminded him that he was not there yet.

"Deal?" He reached out his hand for me to shake it.

I did, and everything stopped. My manager was a real person now, and the consequences of my behavior were just as real.

So, that's why Darla felt so real to my class. Because just a few years before, I was Darla.

Purposeful Storytelling

I told my class that I was making this uncomfortable confession because I wanted them to resist the desire to even the score. Darla is afraid and does not know how to manage her feelings about it. I asked them to remember a time when they feared loss or being invisible or irrelevant. What did they do about it? Firing someone from a large organization for having a "nasty attitude" is rarely a viable strategy. The only real option left is to confront the problem head-on. If you ignore it or try to get rid of it, it will only grow. Fear is contagious, and it will spread. There is no need to tiptoe around Darla's feelings, but I told them they have a responsibility to the company, Darla, their teams, and their own well-being to spend more time considering ways to not only manage the situation, but improve it. Problems do not just melt away. You either fix them or get crushed under their weight.

My intent was to encourage feelings of empathy, but looking back I think I also answered their unspoken question: How do you solve a problem like Darla? You empathize with her and then tackle the issue directly. That looks different for everyone. My manager at the copy center was fed up and confronted me, but there could have been other ways to deal with the situation. That is part of the ambiguity that comes with a manager's responsibility. You do not know how these situations will turn out, but confronting them is the only way to gain some measure of control over the outcome. Letting it fester and potentially spread does a disservice to the problem employee and the rest of the team.

Telling my story was scary and I worried the participants would lose respect for me. That is not what happened. By the second day, people were confessing their own insecurities about being a good manager. One person who had Darla's case study—and had been the most outspoken about Darla's antics—admitted that she thought employees who constantly tested her made her look weak, which was a threat to her career and livelihood. She acknowledged that her anger toward Darla was really about her fear that she was an ineffective leader.

Facilitating With Story

That day, I thought I had nothing to offer because I had no management experience. But I knew that what lurked behind the participants' frustrations were fear, anger, and insecurity—emotions that served as the basis for many of my stories. That is the power of storytelling. You can cut through the content to get to the core of the problem, which is often driven by emotion. This is why facilitators naturally gravitate toward storytelling as a way to connect real-life experiences—and real people—to the content. I still see that course as my instructional design debut, but it was also when I learned the true role of the facilitator and how storytelling can be used as a strategy to do the job well.

You cannot talk about using storytelling to facilitate learning without talking about the art of facilitation itself. When most of the learning and development field's efforts are focused on performance support and online learning, it is easy to lose sight of the facilitator's purpose. We are often given courses (or design them ourselves), along with a directive to take that content and transfer it into people's brains. Ideally, the course we receive is designed to support a learning experience that will help the learner transform knowledge into performance—a performance that will help an organization reach its goals. Facilitators are supposed to guide participants through that learning experience.

"Guide" is a good description of what facilitators do. We are leading participants toward a specific destination, but we recognize that the goal is to help them identify and reach their individual goals—ones that may differ from what we originally planned. Where learners ultimately arrive depends on where they begin and their incentive to adopt new behaviors. Facilitators know the limits of their influence over the outcomes. Janis Chan (2010) writes in *Training Fundamentals: Pfeiffer Essential Guides to Training Basics:* "What trainers sometimes do not realize is that they are not responsible for participants' learning. Participants are responsible for their own learning. The trainer is a guide who is responsible for creating and maintaining an environment in which people are able to learn."

Understanding the facilitator's influence and learning how to use it is essentially mastering the job, which takes time, practice, and study. Practitioners of facilitation learn early that the role is more than a combination of subject matter expertise and public-speaking skills. Yes, those skills are essential, but facilitation also requires empathy and vulnerability, along with the ability to take in information, process it, connect it to course content and previous learner comments, and—and this is mandatory—encourage participants to connect with you as a person. The story I told about being a jerk to my manager probably would have been less successful if I had not built rapport with the participants first. And I would not have felt comfortable being vulnerable in front of them if I did not know that the relationship was already there.

As guides, we help learners make connections, which is at the heart of teaching and learning—a course is simply a series of concepts and tasks connected in ways that are not always obvious. Learners must make connections for themselves between what they are learning and their own experiences. Perhaps through the activities in the course's design, facilitators are fostering connections among the learners so that they can learn from one another as they go through the experience together.

What is an effective way to demonstrate empathy and vulnerability while helping learners make connections? Storytelling! It's one of the oldest teaching devices and remains one of the most effective.

The art of storytelling is a formula that can be practiced and mastered. There is a difference, however, between people who tell stories, regardless of how well they have mastered the formula, and a storyteller. Anyone can tell a story. But to be a storyteller, mastering the formula is not enough. Punchlines are not enough. Recognition is not enough. Telling a recognizable story about a challenge you faced on the job is not as useful if you neglect to dig deeper and move beyond what happened to get to how the incident changed you. While my story was about how I treated my manager and whether my participants recognized that experience, the story's purpose was my realization about why I behaved the way I did and the insight that realization provided.

A Story Teller Versus a Storyteller

Facilitation is not simply about connecting; it is about connecting in the service of change. You may not have considered why an event occurred and what you gained, or lost, as a result. But the desire to reflect on what you have experienced, and then to search for a meaning that can be used to elicit a change in someone else, is the difference between a person who tells stories and a storyteller.

Facilitators who know that the joy of teaching comes with its challenges—the frustration of being face-to-face with learner apathy and resistance, thinking on your feet even when they hurt, working out loud for eight straight hours every day—know that telling stories is not enough. You must select and shape stories that connect and facilitate change. And to get these stories, you must be willing find them and let them find you. You must mine your experiences for meaning and be open to laying what you find bare in front of strangers at a moment's notice. I did not intend to tell my copy center story that day, but I had long ago processed what it meant to me personally and how it influenced my relationships with other managers. I saw the connection between what I learned and who I am today. To facilitate connections, you must first make connections yourself. You need to be a storyteller.

Being a storyteller is a way of life—it is a way of experiencing the world, shaping what you see, and reporting back through the lens of your own context. That storyteller is already inside you; it has been, and will continue, evolving over time. You help that process by knowing how to select, structure, shape, and tell stories that have the greatest capability of facilitating connections and change for listeners.

About This Book

This book is about using storytelling as a facilitation strategy to help course participants make connections to content, ideas, and the people around them through their own experiences. Part 1 makes the case for how stories facilitate learning. It is about those stories that changed both the person who lived them and the person who heard them. We cover the basics of story structure and its importance. Some see storytelling as extemporaneous chats told from memory, but stories are far more likely to be understood and fulfill your intentions if they are purposely shaped with structure. Part 2 focuses on the four characteristics of stories that are most useful for facilitating learning. We will see what each characteristic looks like in practice. You can use these characteristics like a checklist for selecting stories to use when facilitating.

The story itself is nothing without a delivery that helps fulfill your intention. Part 3 is about delivering the stories you have selected and shaped. We will explore the behaviors you can practice as you strengthen the storyteller you already are.

I hope that after reading this book, you will determine that all the rifling through memories and re-examining old victories and failures is worth it. My wish is that you will stop saying you are bad at telling stories and focus on the fact that what you've learned from your experiences is valuable to you and others. While this can be emotional work, I believe that you are patient enough to go through the intellectual exercise of strategically selecting and shaping your stories. I hope that after all the work you put into getting the story right, you deliver it in a manner that enhances the story's power. It all leads to strengthening the natural story-teller inside yourself. Let's go!

PART 1

How Stories Facilitate Learning

Think about the last great story you liked. What did you like about it? Was it unusual? Perhaps it triggered unexpected emotions or brought back memories long forgotten. Now, think about a story that you enjoyed listening to—one where you actually enjoyed the experience of the storyteller bringing the story to life. And has there ever been a story that stayed with you? I do not mean one that you remember. I mean one that stuck to you. You may not have liked the story, and yet it haunted you. You have repeated it so often that people stopped bothering to tell you that you have told them already. It is someone else's story, but the experience of hearing it belongs to you.

There are stories that you liked, stories you enjoyed hearing, and stories you will never forget. But there is a fourth category—stories about change that also change you. Sometimes they are rich, layered, and compelling stories that force your eyes open. They could also be brief—so brief that they break through in a flash like lightning—but are so powerful that they linger long after the strike.

Back when I worked in technical support, I had a co-worker who kept to herself. She had a strong Chinese accent and struggled to communicate in English, which I assumed contributed to her brevity. Once we were in the office alone together, and she asked me if I traveled. I told her I did not like to travel. Back in my late 20s, my philosophy was everything I need to see, I can watch on PBS. She smiled and said:

> "I did not like to travel, and my husband was always wanting to go and see things. Finally, I said yes and then we went to the mountains in Washington and my . . . um. . . ."
>
> She put her hand on her chest and took a quick breath. "It was so beautiful, my heart . . . opened up."

Her story was perfect. It had a challenge to overcome and a change in the protagonist—both necessary ingredients. Most of all, it was simple and honest. Before that moment I had seen travel as just going places and looking at things. But her story changed my mind, and then my mind changed me. She showed me that the joy of travel was in the experience.

Part 1 is about those stories that change both the person who lived it and the person who heard it. They are stories that facilitate learning and, ultimately, change.

1

The Story

o you think you would recognize a story if you heard one? You would be forgiven if you believed that a simple retelling of events was a story. However, it is more than that. Wade Jackson (2011), in his book *Stories at Work,* defines a story as "a sequence of events that progress towards an ending where someone or something has undergone change." In her book *Wired for Story: The Writer's Guide to Using Brain Science to Hook Readers From the Very First Sentence,* Lisa Cron (2012) writes: "A story is how what happens affects someone who is trying to achieve what turns out to be a difficult goal, and how he or she changes as a result."

Both definitions, and others like them, share two terms: *events* and *change.* Unearthing the relevant events requires that you step back and look at the larger picture, while pinpointing the change forces you to look closer and dig deeper.

Something Needs to Happen

A story is a set of connected events, each caused or influenced by the one that came before it. The causal relationships among the events add a forward momentum to the story, which is the secret to compelling the listener to hang on. These connected events lead to a change, which is typically the point of the story, but the change needs to be earned for the listener to get invested.

How is it possible for someone to tell a story where nothing happens? The person telling the story may get stuck in details, or they cannot or have not taken a step back to acknowledge the full sequence of events and reflected on their origins, connections, and influences. For instance, a colleague once told me that she taught a class where a participant read a novel throughout the entire morning, completely ignoring her and the rest of the participants. The participant was not discreet—he held the book up, loudly turned pages, and even reacted to what he was reading. I thought, this is going to be a good story, and I couldn't wait to hear more. Then, she stopped talking.

"Well, what did you do?" I asked.

"About him?"

"Yes. Did you call him out? How did you make him stop?"

"I didn't," she said, like the thought had just occurred to her.

While this may have seemed like a story to her, it was not. It was just a sequence of events. So, how do we transform a sequence of events into a story? Start by identifying the point you want to make with the story you are fleshing out. In my friend's case, the point of the story could be the reason he was reading the book or, considering she may never know the reason, it could have focused on how facilitators should manage the situation. In fact, it could be used to facilitate learning a variety of topics—including train-the-trainer, facilitation, and presentation skills courses. You could also use it for new supervisors who need to learn how to lead and influence in the face of resistance. Picking a point is a key part of framing your intent, which will then influence which events to include.

Once you know what point you are focusing on, you can move on to the events you know and do not know about. Put yourself in her place in the front of that room. I should mention that the book incident took place in the early 2000s, before people multitasked with mobile phones and laptops. Since the rise of the smartphone, I have grown immune to being ignored by a few participants while public speaking, but back then, a person reading a book so brazenly was both unheard of and frankly, bizarre. But while his behavior certainly was not nice and was unusual, who cares? After getting over his unmitigated gall, you'll need to identify more events to make a story out of it. This did not happen in a vacuum. The only way to map out the events that led to a certain point is to look at the larger picture.

Unearthing long-past events may be a challenge. You may not remember them accurately or even at all. Perhaps you remember the events, but not the order or the connections among them. There are contexts in which listing specific events does not matter, but when it does, timelining is a great way to identify event details, their connections, and their meanings.

What Happened? Timelining Key Events

Timelining is a strategy for identifying the events before and after the key event, which is the point of the story. This exercise is designed to help you identify the story's key event and create a timeline of other events that may have come before or after it. The implication is that the events that preceded the key event contributed to its occurrence, and the events that came after it were directly or indirectly caused by it. So, you are specifically looking for events that will support your intention and the causal relationships among them. To determine whether an event will work, you must consider its significance.

Begin timelining by hand drawing a line that represents the story (Figure 1-1). Then identify the key event, which is probably the part that makes you remember the story so well. It is usually the point on which the rest of the story depends. Writers may call it the climax, which is part of the pyramid-shaped, dramatic structure model. Starting on the left, you begin with the exposition, followed by rising tension, which is represented by the left wall of the pyramid. The rising tension leads to the narrative's climax, which sits atop the pyramid and is where dramatic tension is at its highest point. After the climax, we move down the right side of the pyramid with falling tension, ending with the resolution. Writers have challenged, reimagined, and outright defied this structure over time (for example, leading with the climax, having no resolution, and so forth), but it is a helpful model to consider when timelining story events. We will use the pyramid structure as an influence here and begin by placing the key event near the middle of the timeline.

Figure 1-1. How to Begin Timelining

Story

Key Event

Now, starting with the key event, search your memory and find as many events that preceded the key event as possible. Remember, you are looking for events that both support your intention and have a causal relationship with the key event. It is easier to begin with events that you remember happening immediately before the key event and work backward through time. We call these leading events because they are events that led to the key event.

Once you are confident that you've identified all the leading events, move on to the consequential events. These are the events that occurred as a result of the key event (and all the events that led up to the key event). It is important to stay focused on your intent as you identify consequential events. Avoid overreaching by attributing the cause of circumstantial incidents to the key event. Also, concentrate on what happened as opposed to what did not happen. It is often impossible to say that an event did not occur because of something else. For example, saying, "And because of that one interaction, my boss promoted me to manager," is more believable than, "And because of that one interaction, my boss did not promote me to manager." The first is the inspirational ending we are used to, which may give your assumption credibility. The second is less credible, and may make people wonder whether you are leaving out another reason you did not get promoted.

An essential part of timelining is self-questioning, which helps you remember leading and consequential events and consider the connections among them. There are no specific questions to ask, but the types of questions fall into three categories:

- sequence and connections
- place and time
- insight.

For every event that meets your criteria, draw a vertical line in the appropriate place on the timeline (Figure 1-2).

Figure 1-2. Adding Events to the Timeline

Story

Leading Events   **Key Event**   **Consequential Events**

What follows is an example of a timelining exercise. I'll start by explaining my intention for the story because, as I mentioned earlier, intention fuels the timelining process.

The Night Emails

Intention: The goal of the story is to warn a group of managers in a supervisory class about the possible consequences of off-hour communication with their direct reports and to encourage the managers to cease or minimize the practice.

What I remember: I managed a team of five people. The days were busy, so I sent most of my emails at night. It seemed like, no matter when I sent an email, I would get an immediate response. I assumed they were just at their computers or on their BlackBerries and, like me, thought they would get a head start on the next workday by answering emails immediately. During a meeting, I told my manager that I had received some information the night before from one of my direct reports. He told me that I should not email my employees in the evening because they may feel obligated to answer me back immediately. He told me to consider waiting until the next day or using Outlook's delay send feature. I thought his request was silly because I never told my team when to reply. They were making the choice to do so. I also did not take him seriously because he sent me emails all night long. I stopped sending emails at night for a little while, but soon started again.

The description of this initial memory is how stories may sound when they are only a sequence of events with no insight, agency, or acknowledged change in the protagonist. Timelining helps fill in the blanks with events, and then connecting those events leads to deeper reflection.

Timelining Questions

Key Event: Meeting With My Manager

- **Sequence and connections**
  - What happened immediately before the meeting? *I don't remember.*
  - What instigated the meeting? *I do recall that we were in the midst of a large, stressful project. I imagine the meeting was a "check-in" meeting and not specifically about the emails.*
  - What happened after the meeting? *I do not remember, but if I were to guess, I probably went to a co-worker's desk to complain about my manager's request. And I am sure I focused on the fact that he sent me emails at night despite him telling me not to send them.*

- **Place and time**
  - Where was the meeting held? *It was on-site in a conference room.*
  - How long had he been your manager prior to this incident? *I worked there for a little over a year, and I believe this happened about halfway through my tenure.*

- **Insight**
  - How did you feel about your relationship with your manager? *We had a tense relationship and struggled to communicate with each other effectively.*

- How did you feel about your team? *I was new to managing a team of that size, so I was learning as I went along. I liked everyone, but I was unsure about how they felt about me.*
- Why did you really send emails at night? *Honestly, I did not want the answers to come back to me immediately. I wanted the problems off my plate for a while. I was initially surprised to receive replies—it was the first job I'd had where people were sending and answering emails at night. It was frustrating when I received immediate answers because I would have to think about the problem again before I went to bed.*
- How did you feel (before and after the meeting) about your boss sending you emails at night? *Before the meeting, it bothered me, but it seemed to be part of the culture. After the meeting, the hypocrisy bothered me even more.*
- The focus right now seems to be on his hypocrisy. Does that theme serve your intent? *No. I suppose the point I could focus on is the importance of ensuring that you model the behaviors you want to see in your staff, but that is a story for another day. I want to get back to my own behavior.*
- Take a further step back and put the focus on yourself as a manager who is now teaching other managers. Did the conversation with your manager give you any insight into the consequences of off-hours communication? *I did not want to admit it then, but my manager was right. I know he was right because I answered every email he sent me at night. He did not ask me to reply, but I felt obligated to anyway. It didn't matter that he was doing what he told me not to do—I was blinded by my negative thoughts toward him. What mattered was that I did not want to send my staff into a tailspin at the end of the evening. I knew the consequences of my choices because I was living them, and I did not want my team to feel like I did.*

I will stop there. Taking a closer look at a simple story about emailing my staff at night turned into an exploration of my own insecurities as a new manager. Additional events and new insights appeared because of the questioning process. Now, let's walk through the timeline I constructed for this story.

Constructing the Timeline

Leading events:

1. I am hired as a new manager at a company where off-hours communication seems like the norm, a concept that was new to me; as a result. . . .
2. I begin sending emails to my staff at night and, honestly, I was fine doing this because I did not want immediate replies. I was still new and unsure of myself and the decisions I was making; as a result. . . .
3. When I received a response to an email I sent to an employee late at night, I mentioned it to my manager during our meeting; as a result. . . .

Key event:

4. My manager told me that I was potentially causing anxiety within my team, and that I should consider stopping the behavior; as a result. . . .

Consequential events:

5. I was angry with my manager because he sent me emails at night, too. I chose to focus on his hypocrisy instead of changing my behavior; as a result. . . .
6. Every time he sent me an email at night, my focus on his behavior made me realize the impact the nightly emails had on me; as a result. . . .
7. I had to admit to myself that my emails were having the same effect on my team that my manager's emails were having on me.

By taking a few steps back and looking at the bigger picture using timelining, I was able to piece together a more robust story with the events that led up to the key event and were then caused by it. The timeline sets you up nicely for the other element that's included in most definitions of *story:* Something or someone must change.

What Is "Change"?

To better understand the role of events and change in stories, look to the cinema. I am a movie buff. Not the type with an encyclopedic memory of titles, dates, and lines—but I love how movies expand my perception and knowledge of human behavior and what drives it.

An essential element of every movie is the protagonist's character arc, which maps a character's journey through a film. Character arcs are usually described using the events in a character's journey and the changes that come as a result of those events. Many films are based on a character's journey: good girl gone bad, the prodigal son returns, road movie as metaphor for self-discovery—you get the idea. Change is often the central plot point of classic horror films, whether it is the physical transformation from man to monster or the spiritual transformation from monster to man. And change is not just for fiction. Many successful documentaries feature people who were changed by events—or who forced the world around them to change instead. Movies attempt to investigate, reveal, and document change and wrap it into a narrative for consumption.

But remember, we are not just talking about change for change's sake. Writers talk about characters "earning" a change. At the end of my story about the night emails, I could have simply said, "And after my manager told me to stop writing emails at night, I stopped and was a changed woman." Perhaps, but that is not helpful to anyone but me. What is helpful is seeing the change in my choices over time, or rather, to see me earning the change. It is that process, rather than the change itself, that learners connect with. Your experience may instruct learners on how to make the same change.

Turning back to film as an example, consider the movie montage. The boxer can't just win a fight. We have to witness him earning it. The stronger we relate to the character, the more willing we are to put ourselves in his shoes. You, too, can transform your body, win back your wife, and prepare to beat the world heavyweight champion in five minutes! Suspension of disbelief aside, the same principle that applies to audiences watching *Rocky* applies to a new manager hearing your story about how you learned the importance of giving feedback the hard way. That is how change functions in a story, and it is one reason that stories are such great facilitation tools. A sequence of events without a change can be a story, but it won't be a particularly interesting, compelling, or motivating one. You need to find the change.

Finding the Change

Finding *events* forces you to step back and look at the larger picture, while finding a *change* forces you to look closer and dig deeper. It is easy to see storytelling as a series of events, because telling the story is the only visible manifestation of a long and complicated process. And it is one of the easiest steps. The hard part is experiencing the events, allocating space and time (literally and figuratively) to gain perspective on them, shaping them into a story, and knowing when and how to tell it.

Doug Stevenson is a strategic business storyteller who has trained professionals in storytelling for years. In his book, *Doug Stevenson's Story Theater Method: Strategic Storytelling in Business* (2011), he writes that "the speakers and storytellers who make the most enduring impact on their audiences have one thing in common: they possess insight—the ability to look inside and find a profound truth. They see what everyone sees and choose to go deeper."

Some see little value in going deeper to explore seemingly meaningless occurrences, and even fewer people want to revisit and examine unpleasant events. I do not blame my colleague for not wanting to further examine why a participant read a book in her class while she was talking, let alone explore its deeper meaning. It is probably better for her to move beyond that experience and accept that whatever happened had nothing to do with her. It is the best way to protect yourself. She would probably classify what happened as just one of those "toss-away" anecdotes, which are retellings of memories about inconsequential events. And yet, the only reason I knew about the book incident was because she told me about it. And she could only tell me about it because she remembered it. Because you are more likely to remember incidents that affected you in some way, his actions may have been more consequential than she realized. You're not going to vividly remember and repeat events that are really "no big deal."

The toss-away stories that we remember carry more weight than we think, and the keys to why we react the way we do to certain stimuli could be locked away inside them. Storytellers are committed to searching their pasts for changes and their causes. But it takes time and experience to know when going too deep is pointless. Indeed, there is a point of diminishing returns when you go so deep into the tangled roots that you lose perspective on what is connected. That's why so much of storytelling depends on making direct connections between your intent and what is included in the story. Events, although open for interpretation, are real—they can be witnessed, documented, and verified. Therefore, it's easier to build a formula for finding them, one that can be applied to different contexts. Change, however, is more elusive—it may not be real at all. If it's not witnessed by anyone other than the person doing the changing, verification is almost impossible, and it's difficult to apply a strategy or formula to it. I only know of one way: Look for the truth.

Banging on the Lid

Do you consider the change you are looking for and then find the story that fits? Or, do you find the story and then find the change that occurred because of it? The answer is both—do not make it harder than it is. If an incident that happened years ago stands out in your memory, then it may have some significance. Significant events tend to have a lingering impact on our lives, which is typically followed by a change in deed or perception. But you will only see it if you are willing to see what is true about the person you were before and after the experience. And you will only bring out that inner storyteller once you are willing to talk about it.

We tend to stuff our toss-away stories into jars and store them away in our memories. We often forget they are there, but we can feel their weight and are keenly aware of the space they occupy. Over time, as vague memories that once seemed inconsequential become useful, the jar's now corroded lid becomes harder to twist off. You may have to bang on the lid of the jar to get to what is inside. In lieu of a strategic formula to uncover the truth about how an incident changed you, I suggest you do just that: Bang on that lid with questions until the lid opens up.

Using "The Night Emails" story as an example, here are some of the questions I used to get started thinking:

- What did I feel about my behavior after my discussion with my manager?
- How does that differ from how I felt before?
- Was the change out of character for me? Was I surprised by it?
- What does how I felt before and after the discussion say about me as a manager? What does it say about me as a person?
- Did the change benefit me? Did it benefit anyone else?

Each question moves you closer to what's inside the jar: What is really at the core of those stories? What does it reveal about what's true for me and others? In other words, if you are looking for stories, follow the truth.

Following the Truth to the Story

This book is not about my stories. I use them as examples of how I have transformed the events that have shaped my life and career into facilitation tools. You may be wondering how to find interesting and applicable stories from your life. What if you are a young professional just starting your career and don't think any of your stories would provide any insight to a person 10 years your senior? What if you are close to retirement, but think your experiences from years ago aren't relatable to today's young professionals? What if you believe your career and life have been uneventful, and so your stories are boring? While there is no good answer for any of these questions, my advice is to follow the truth—it always leads to a story.

When I studied writing, we talked about *Truth* with a "big T" and *truth* with a "small t." The implication is that "big T" truths are objectively true—the sky is blue and the grass is green. "Small t" truths are true for you because you experienced them, but are subjective in that they may not be true for everyone else. "Small t" truths are not only opinions. Opinions are views or judgments that are not necessarily based on fact or knowledge. "Small t" truths are factual experiences you have been through, and are consequently influenced and filtered by your worldview. The best stories are a balance of "Ts" and "ts." Now, where do you find them?

Where Do Stories Come From?

All your stories will come from one of two places: events or relationships (Stevenson 2011). Wade Jackson, in his 2011 book *Stories at Work*, categorizes four story sources—your professional career, the people in your life, the events in your life, and your values—and lists the questions needed to bang on that lid. I've summarized them here and included a few comments of my own:

1. **Reflect on your professional career:** The experiences you enjoyed the most and the least, mistakes you made and what you learned from them, your major professional accomplishments, who helped or hurt your career, and your major turning points and their effect.

2. **Reflect on people in your life:** People who had a positive impact on you throughout your life (for example, teachers, friends, co-workers, managers, mentors, and mentees), people you admire and why, people who triggered emotions (such as love, envy, hate, and fear), and people who taught you something about yourself.

3. **Reflect on events in your life:** Times when you overcame great odds, your proudest achievements, events that triggered happiness or fear (or both), trips you've taken, childhood memories and what you learned from them, or memorable events while engaging in hobbies or other interests.

4. **Reflect on your values:** Times when your values were reinforced or compromised, times when you've experienced great kindness (or extended it), times when you learned to trust (or not to), times when you felt guilty about what you did or didn't do.

A way to find stories is to identify the origin of the change your story describes. The classic model for the origin story is the superhero narrative, which hinges on transformation and will serve the same purpose as the stories you are looking for. Origin stories provide a guideline for story selection because they tell the legend of how you became who you are today. We are all shaped by our experiences, and our stories (and scars) are the proof that we not only triumphed, but also learned and grew from them. Just don't forget to balance objective truths with your subjective ones.

Wrap-Up: The Story on Stories

A story has two key components: events and change. Begin with identifying the point of the story and then identify the key event that made the point possible. Perhaps the key event is meeting with someone who eventually led to you experiencing a life-changing revelation—in that case, the revelation that is the point of your story. After the key event, use timelining to flesh out your story by identifying the events that led to the key event and the ones that were caused by that event.

Timelining helps you find events by encouraging you to question what you remember, and to think more deeply about how each step may have led to the one that followed. Select events for the timeline by identifying the connections between them. In other words, only include events that have a causal relationship. Identifying these connected events and how they ultimately led to a revelation or change are the first steps in transforming an ordinary sequence of events into a story that may help facilitate the type of performance you are looking for.

2

Storytelling and Facilitating Performance

n those days when the weather is changing at a moment's notice or the sun and the shade seem to be in two different seasons, I often think of Aesop's fable "Northern Wind and the Sun." In the fable, the wind and the sun make a bet on who is the stronger of the two. They decide to settle the matter by seeing who can make a nearby traveler remove his coat—the wind's wild force or the steady pressure of the sun. The wind causes the traveler to wrap his coat tighter, but the warmth of the sun makes the man to take the coat off—the sun wins! The moral of the story: "Gentleness and kind persuasion win where force and bluster fail."

Aesop's fables are clear examples of stories intended to influence behavior. Fairy tales are also morality tales whose purpose are to shape behavior and perception. While many fairy tales have unknown origins, and others have been softened in approach and message over time, they still serve the same function—to wrap a message in a palatable coating so that it is easier to swallow.

Using stories to influence is a common strategy. Executives and business veterans often tell stories about their experiences and the hard-won lessons they learned along the way. Stories are an indispensable tool for building corporate culture and making values clear. Yet despite their power and longevity, stories remain underused as a facilitation strategy in corporate learning. I feel comfortable making such a claim because I see it—or rather, do not see it. In the training courses I take in person and online, many facilitators make little effort to connect their personal experiences to the content. When I observe train-the-trainer courses as I prepare to redesign them at several different companies each year, I see very few stories shared about actual application.

I know facilitators may not have stories to share if they are delivering courses in topics where they have no experience with the tasks. And I know others are simply not interested in facilitating with stories because they believe it wastes time. After all, we often work with analytical people who only have a few hours to spare. They just want to know what to do.

Whether you embrace the power of storytelling or are ambivalent about its place in your toolbox, it is difficult to deny its effectiveness in reinforcing memory and, consequently, learning. In his book *Advanced Presentations by Design: Creating Communication That Drives Action*, Andrew Abela (2013) links story to memory and learning:

> Stories are fundamental to how we think, learn, and make sense
> of the world around us. Storytelling has been present in every
> age of human history and in every civilization and culture.
> Stories appear to enable understanding and memory, and much
> of both child and adult learning appears to be acquired through
> a story format. One important reason that stories are so
> powerful is that information delivered through stories is more
> memorable. Memory is strengthened by linking information
> together, and stories link information in multiple ways. Also,
> stories engage the emotions, and this too aids memory.

This chapter provides an overview of the ways that storytelling facilitates learning and performance. Training can only influence knowledge, skills, or attitudes (KSAs)—all of which affect performance. We will focus on how storytelling can drive each one.

Storytelling for Knowledge

What does it mean to "know"? We usually consider knowledge to be an enabling objective instead of a terminal one because we cannot observe knowledge. It is "baked" into the performance goal we want learners to achieve. The assumption is that you haven't mastered a performance unless you "know" the facts that support it.

We can, however, observe people *using* knowledge. We can "see" that people understand a concept because they can describe, explain, or identify it. Often, this base performance is all we need, or can hope for. We cannot force people to manage their teams fairly and equitably, but we can assess whether people know how their organization defines "fairly and equitably," and that they know the implications of noncompliance. In the book *How Learning Works: Seven Research-Based Principles for Smart Teaching*, the authors write that how learners organize knowledge influences how they learn and apply what they know (Ambrose et al. 2010). As we explore storytelling and knowledge, we will focus on how three strategies can help learners adopt knowledge: organization, context, and patterns.

Organization: How Order and Structure Choice Facilitate Learning

Content organization is one of the primary focuses of my work in instructional design. I move content around and attempt to structure it to make the best impact. Whether I teach the whole task (or end result) first and then break it down into parts, or teach the parts as they culminate in the whole task, depends on the content, the learning situation, and what the learners currently know. For example, if the whole task is procedural with a set of fixed steps, it may be better to focus on the parts first. If the whole task is strategic and the learners can choose from a variety of paths to completion, understanding the destination first may be crucial.

Content organization strategies can also be used to facilitate connections. It is important to help learners make connections between what they already know about a subject and the new content. Suppose you are facilitating a class on coaching strategies to a group of managers. You may want to make connections between the management role and the coaching role by comparing them or explaining how they complement one another.

Stories are content organization tools. I once taught a course that opened with a problem presented as a story. After engaging the learners in discussion, they soon wanted to know the answer. However, the answer was the "change" that occurred, which they'd only understand if we continued the discussion. Throughout the course, we revisited the story. Each time, the learners were able to step into the role of the protagonist armed with what they had just learned. This pattern continued to the end of the course, at which point they were able to find their own answers. Because the content and the stories were organized in a manner that reflected real life, the story and the content together facilitated transfer.

Context: How Context Adds Meaning to Stories

Years ago, when I was an employee in a training department, it surprised me how many people would run up to the training center's receptionist five minutes before classes were to begin and breathlessly ask what class they were supposed to attend. Not the classroom location—the class itself. Their managers just told them to go to training that day at 8:30 a.m. This was before we had learning management systems, so the receptionist would have to either rattle off class names to see if any rang a bell or scour a massive Microsoft Excel spreadsheet until she found the student's name and a corresponding class.

The real challenge in these situations is for the facilitator, who has to teach a participant who has no idea why they are enrolled in the course. As you facilitate throughout the day, you can almost see your words flying past the participant's head, never quite hitting the mark. I believe that making content relevant is not solely the facilitator's burden, but when your learners have little to no context for what you are teaching and what it may mean for them, it is difficult to avoid the responsibility of having to make the content matter. Context is important because learners need to know how the content fits into their work lives. According to the authors of *How Learning Works: Seven Research-Based Principles for Smart Teaching*,

"Do not assume that because students have learned a skill that they will automatically know where or when to apply it. It is important to clearly and explicitly explain the contexts in which particular skills are—or are not—applicable" (Ambrose et al. 2010).

Stories work well for theories that are context dependent. Suppose you are facilitating a communication skills course and you are discussing being intentional about the purpose of your messages. The goal is for the learners to consider the utility of the message before they frame it, but part of doing that requires understanding the context of the message—whom you are sending it to, when you are sending it, what information is already known, and so forth. The facilitator can share the idea behind intention, tell stories with varying contextual elements, and then have the learners apply the key principle repeatedly with different outcomes based on the context.

Patterns: How Recognizing Patterns Leads to Learning

I used to teach a management course at a nearby community college. Many of my students were supervisors and were happy to contribute knowledge they'd learned from experience. One of these students often focused on the worst that could happen. If I said that giving feedback is the best way to communicate expectations, she'd say, "Yeah, but they won't listen." If I said encouraging intrinsic motivation can help ensure employees stay focused when you're not around, she'd say, "If you're not watching, they won't do it. Period."

Once I asked her whether her employees knew she felt this way about their work efforts. She said they did because she told them all the time. Soon after delivering this feedback, they would do exactly what she predicted they would do. She was right! It was clear that she didn't see the pattern: telling people that they were doing a bad job often resulted in them doing a bad job. I told the group a story about a job I had in high school:

> When I was in high school, I worked at a fast food restaurant in Highland Park, Michigan. It was my first job. The assistant manager was tough and intimidating. To her, I was a snob

who thought I was too good to work there. She was always hovering over me, making me second guess every move. She let me work the cash register, but never the drive-thru. Only the best and the brightest got to work the drive-thru. As I spent my days ringing up two-piece dinners and passing them to customers in the lobby through bulletproof-glass doors that required cashier-customer coordination to open, she kept warning me not to mess up. Naturally, I messed up. It wouldn't even occur to me to do something incorrectly until she told me *not* to do it incorrectly. I put up with her for a year and then I went off to college.

The summer after freshman year, I went back to work at the restaurant for a few weeks. During that first week, the drive-thru cashier got sick. The assistant manager had no choice. She put me in the game. I was nervous, but the manager seemed too tired to lurk over by me like she used to.

Well, in a few days, I got the hang of the drive-thru. Then, I got good at it. And finally, I nailed it. Near the end of my time there, the assistant manager, like a cliché from a sports movie where the underdog wins the game, said, "What happened to you?" I knew that was her way of saying, "Good job."

I told this story to illustrate a pattern for my students, but from the employee's point of view. My manager's constant doubting made me doubt myself, and it was a trigger-response pattern that happened repeatedly. I doubt that one year in college contributed to making me a better drive-thru cashier, but I did gain confidence and had a better understanding of my abilities. I was less intimidated by the assistant manager, and the pattern was broken. Stories help learners see patterns, and in this case, it was one of the simplest patterns around—the relationship between cause and effect.

Storytelling for Skills

Learning objectives all have the same purpose—facilitate knowledge so that learners can use it to demonstrate skills. We want learners to move from theories to practical usage quickly. However, stories, no matter how truthful, are hypothetical because while the situation happened to the storyteller, it may never happen to the learner in the same way with the same outcome. So, how does storytelling facilitate learning practical skills when stories are, by their nature, theories on possible outcomes? In this section, we'll talk about three ways facilitators can use the hypothetical to drive the practical: demonstrations, practice, and feedback.

Demonstrations: Show and Tell

I began my career facilitating software courses. I believed that my job was simply to tell the participants how to use the software, but what I did instead was explain the screen to them, covering each button and menu item. It was what I now call the "Z" format—start in the upper-left corner and move your way right, covering all the icons and menu items; then move down the screen to the center to cover the primary interface; and then, finally, cover whatever is on the bottom status bar from left to right again.

I later realized that my job was not to teach people how to use the software. It was to teach them how to do their jobs using the software. The "Z" format does not accomplish this, but demonstrating tasks in the context of a story can help.

I still teach software courses, but I find it far more enjoyable to teach software I have personal experience using because it allows me to tell relevant stories. For example, when I teach new e-learning developers how to use the tools to design and publish modules, it is easy to focus too heavily on the software's features and neglect to mention the practical use of each. If you are not careful, you may end up spending the day rattling off a bunch of "you can do this or that" statements. Your participants will leave familiar with a bunch of individual features, but not be able to complete any one full task.

I use stories to facilitate software demonstrations. The software used to complete a specific task is the "change" that drives the story. Instead of beginning a lesson on how to create master slides in PowerPoint with, "Now, we are going to learn how to create master slides in

PowerPoint," you begin with the story about what triggers the need for master slides, and how learning how to create and manage them is the solution to the problem.

Practice: Let the Learner Take the Wheel

In any course, there will be participants at a variety of skill levels. No story you tell will resonate with everyone. I have worked in several different environments, but when I teach learning and development courses, my colleagues and participants tell me about the technical constraints they work under and it still surprises me. Some of the lessons I share are simply not applicable given the limitations of the technology they have at their disposal.

Whenever I experience a strong disconnect between my experience and that of my participants, I remember that facilitating with stories does not mean only sharing instructor stories. Always encourage participants to share their stories, too. Before beginning to teach a task, ask participants to stop and think of a practical problem that the skill you are teaching could resolve. Encourage them to move beyond the general examples you provide and get specific using their own context. Ask them to visualize their own stories as they try to make sense of each step in the process.

Feedback: Make It Part of the Story

While learners are practicing skills, giving feedback is essential. It is one of my favorite uses of storytelling while facilitating. When we think of feedback, we usually consider it the end of something—a learner completes a task, the facilitator provides feedback, and they both move on. But when facilitating with story, there is no right answer; there are only the consequences of a choice, which is also part of the story. It is a missed opportunity to stop there without encouraging the learners to further explore the choices they will have to make while choosing to use or actually using a skill.

Let's use a coaching example again. Suppose you have a four-step coaching model, and one step is to have an honest conversation about the behaviors the coach has observed by watching the coachee. The model gives you a step-by-step strategy for how to approach these discussions, which you walk through with your learners with the assumption that it will work and the conversation will go smoothly. The skill you are teaching is to use the strategy, not necessarily to teach managers how to have real conversations with real people with real problems. You can remedy that by putting this in the context of a story and tossing in the curveballs that happen in real life.

I ask the group, "What's the second step?"

They dutifully repeat, "Have an open and honest conversation about what behaviors you're observing."

Instead of moving on, I say, "What if the coachee rejects your open honesty?"

Participants will either look up in surprise that I strayed from what they thought was the script or look down to avoid being called out.

One volunteer says, "You don't make it personal. You make it about what you've observed. They can't argue with that."

I say, "OK. I'm your coachee and I am indeed arguing with that. You don't see me every day. You can only be making assumptions about my behaviors."

The participant flashes a nervous grin, wondering how far I'm going to take this. I don't smile back. I become his coachee and he needs to do something about this escalating confrontation. The model for the conversation is right in front of him in the workbook, but he doesn't use it.

Another participant, looking at the model mumbles an answer, "If you meet resistance. . . ."

"Yes?" I say.

She continues reading, "If you meet resistance, you should concede some control back to the coachee by getting clarity on what they disagree with and why."

Now, if I had simply blown past that part of the model, we would have never known that using it is not as easy as it seems. Use feedback to enhance your stories and ensure that learners fully understand the skill they are intended to adopt.

Storytelling for Attitude

I often design and facilitate courses with objectives that may require an attitude change for the participant. I have always been reluctant to suggest that any training I have designed or delivered had the power to change someone's way of thinking. Surely, I have broadened a perspective or two, but I can barely change my own way of thinking, let alone someone else's.

We know that a facilitated workshop can support a larger performance solution; however, training is often not a solution on its own. Countless factors play a role in whether an attitude adjustment is going to occur, such as the learner's current disposition, management support, and the work environment. Further, similar to how knowledge is considered baked into a skill, attitude is also baked in—sort of. Some skills cannot be mastered unless there's an underlying belief system in place. Change management is an example of this. Some believe that when a change comes, you just accept it and there is no need for hand-holding. Others, especially those who work in acquisition-prone industries (banking, telecommunications, and so forth), know from experience that unmanaged change can lead to inefficiencies, resentment, and perhaps a mass exodus. It is difficult to master change management if you do not believe that change can and should be managed.

My approach to designing for and facilitating topics that require an attitude change is to focus on how certain perspectives can influence the way a skill is performed. Essentially, while you can perform a task based on an ideology you do not believe in, it is difficult to do it well. This is where facilitating with story can shine because stories can trigger empathy, which is often the key to changing a perspective. Rather than strategies, I use cautionary tales and personal testimonials to facilitate attitude changes. Both have qualities that can help broaden or focus perspectives and contribute to the outcome you are looking for.

Cautionary Tales: Beware All Who Tread Here!

A cautionary tale is a story intended to warn the listener against engaging in a specific behavior under the threat that it will not end well. I remember growing up in the 1970s and 1980s and being in a state of constant high-alert, courtesy of school screenings about rampant drug use, the TV series *ABC Afterschool Specials* that made you too scared to leave the house or stay at home, and heavy-handed "very special episodes" of your favorite television shows, where new characters appeared out of nowhere for the sole purpose of being subjected to a censor-approved version of a tragedy.

The point of a cautionary tale is to affect behavior by tapping into emotions. The fear or empathy these stories trigger may cause viewers to re-examine their values or change them. Cautionary tales are a strategy to encourage listeners to think about outcomes they didn't consider initially. You are not teaching that a specific outcome is guaranteed to occur if the learner performs a task in a certain way. You are teaching that the best strategy is to consider as many possible outcomes within reason.

Alternatively, cautionary tales can be seen as pessimistic and undermining. For example, a participant explains one way to handle a situation only to have the facilitator swoop in to say, "At one company I worked for, we did what you suggested—we reduced the number of employees working each shift—and robberies immediately went up. We realized that we put our employees in a position where their sites were more likely to get robbed because they were too large for the few employees to be aware of their surroundings." No manager wants to hear that, especially if it's an action they've already taken. Like many strategies, cautionary tales can be great learning tools if used properly. Do not assume learners know your intentions.

Personal Stories: Can We Talk?

I once attended a train-the-trainer course where the trainer asked if we told personal stories while we facilitated. I had assumed that we all told personal stories when we facilitate, but I soon noticed that I was the only one nodding. The consensus among the group appeared to be that personal stories had no place in training. However, the facilitator told us that participants want to hear our stories. They are there to learn from both the content and our experiences.

The word *personal* was the source of the disconnect. What makes a story "personal"? Our class discussion made me consider my definition of the word. I suppose the first thing that comes to mind is that a personal story is about an event that happens in your personal life—for example, at the beach or at home with your family. It is true that I have sat through courses where facilitators told bizarre, irrelevant, and, sometimes, inappropriate stories that left me scratching my head. If we define "personal" that way, then I agree. And while I felt like this is all obvious, again, I have seen the line get crossed repeatedly. The error here, however, is not the use of personal stories—it is the use of poor judgment.

In a professional context, "personal" stories only include relevant events that happened to the storyteller personally that provide insight and context for learners. Real life is rarely as clean-cut as the content. Stories describing a personal experience with the subject matter are ideal for facilitating to influence attitude. Emotions and ideologies can make real life messy, so what better way to facilitate a change than by using real life?

Wrap-Up: The ABCs of Storytelling KSAs

The purpose of any teaching strategy is to facilitate performance. This chapter discussed how storytelling does just that by exploring the components of performance that training can influence: knowledge, skills, and attitudes.

Storytelling helps learners absorb new knowledge by providing a framework for organizing content, putting content into context, and illustrating patterns. Stories can enhance demonstrations, practice, and feedback as learners adopt new skills. Storytelling can also influence learner attitudes through cautionary tales and personal stories.

3

Shaping Your Stories

uppose you are an experienced call center professional tasked with facilitating a customer service course. You are in the "managing customer expectations" section, and you want to tell a story about an incident that occurred back when you worked on the front lines taking calls. Six events occurred in your story:

1. The customer called in after receiving a defective item.
2. The customer was not able to provide the information you needed to look up the order.
3. The customer became annoyed and started yelling at you.
4. You became frustrated and yelled back.
5. The call escalated, and you were asked to meet with your manager.
6. Your manager coached you on strategies that you could use to avoid similar situations in the future.

If you told this story in chronological order, listeners may be distracted wondering where the story was going, but it would add to the suspense. If you started the story in the middle by saying, "Have you ever been so frustrated with a customer that you yelled back?" listeners will know what to expect, but having that information in advance may diminish the story's impact. Perhaps you could begin with the end and say, "If you've ever been in a situation where you wanted to yell at a customer, I have a few strategies that could help. Let me tell you how I learned about them." Learners would know what to listen for, but depending on how you tell the story, they may struggle to distinguish what actually happened from what you learned. Or, what if you removed events? What if you did not mention the first event—that the issue was the company's fault? How would that change the story?

The secret to a story's effectiveness is its structure. Structure controls how the story's content is delivered to the listener, so it affects how your story's content and intent will be understood. A story's structure includes two components: the frame and the content the frame holds. Each part has its own value and lends support to the other. It's important to discuss structure first, because influences the stories you select.

This last chapter in part 1 focuses on framing, and content is the focus of part 2. First, I'll discuss two common structures to give you a clearer idea about how structures function. Then, I'll describe what I use. I am not advocating a specific model because what you use will depend on your preferences and your intent.

Story structure models typically fall in two categories: recipe models and building blocks models. Recipe models explain what a good story includes. They dictate what should be added and how it should taste, and, as with recipes, each ingredient influences the taste of the entire meal. Building blocks models focus on structure—you arrange story element in a specific order, but the content decisions are yours.

Recipe Model: The Hero's Journey

Classic narratives tend to categorize people as heroes or villains. While stories have evolved to allow for more complex archetypes like the anti-hero, many books and movies still use the never-ending battle between good and evil as a framework. Every story where the hero saves the day rests on the foundation of another story about how the hero came to be. Writers and philosophers long ago discovered that these transformations, examples of which trace all the way back to mythology, had been described in remarkably similar ways. This theory was popularized in Joseph Campbell's book *The Hero with a Thousand Faces* (1949). Campbell describes what he calls a monomyth, defined as "a universal pattern that is the essence of, and common to, heroic tales in every culture."

The monomyth, otherwise known as the hero's journey, is essentially a character arc, which is the transformation all characters experience throughout a narrative. It's also a good example of a recipe model. The 12-step model is used as a structure for stories that feature or are influenced by the transformation of a protagonist (or hero). Each step describes what the protagonist experiences on the journey from their current identity to becoming a hero. It's similar to the timelining exercise in chapter 1, in that it pinpoints a series of crucial events that lead to a change.

The hero's journey is structured as follows:

1. **Ordinary world:** This shows the hero's current life. It's used to help create contrast with the special world the hero is about to enter. A good example of this is *The Wizard of Oz* because the story begins with Dorothy's life in Kansas.

2. **Call to adventure:** The hero is presented with a problem or challenge that must be taken on. After the call, the hero can no longer stay comfortably in the ordinary world. This is a crucial plot point in books and movies—the detective gets a new case, the criminal agrees to do one last job, Luke Skywalker sees Princess Leia's message.

3. **Refusal of the call:** The hero is reluctant to cross the threshold to follow through on the call, requiring some other influence—perhaps a person or an event—to encourage them to take on the challenge, like Obi Wan Kenobi's requests of Luke Skywalker, which Luke initially refuses.

4. **Meeting with the mentor:** The mentor helps the hero prepare to face the challenge. The mentor encourages, teaches, and guides—but ultimately the hero must face the challenge alone. Examples of mentors include Glinda the Good Witch and Mr. Miyagi from *The Karate Kid*.

5. **Crossing the threshold:** Here the hero crosses over from the ordinary world to the special world, where adventure awaits. This is the point in the story where the action begins—Dorothy heads down the Yellow Brick Road.

6. **Tests, allies, and enemies:** After crossing the threshold, the hero is tested repeatedly and meets allies and enemies along the way—Dorothy is accompanied by allies the Scarecrow, the Tin Man, and the Lion, and is chased by flying monkeys who serve as enemies. This stage allows us to see the character learn, grow, and begin to make the changes required to successfully overcome the primary challenge further down the line.

7. **Approach to the inmost cave:** The hero enters a dangerous place that is usually the lair of their enemy. Here is where they use their wit to get past guards and traps to come face-to-face with their greatest fear (or enemy)—Luke squares off against Darth Vader.

8. **Central ordeal:** The hero reaches the enemy and the battle begins. The important part here is that the hero dies or appears to die so that they can be reborn anew. This is the "There's no way out. Oh look! Here's a way out," plot point in every action film. In *The Matrix,* Neo decides to head back into the Matrix to rescue Morpheus.

9. **Reward:** The hero survives death and is rewarded either literally or figuratively for their efforts. Sometimes the reward is a magic sword or just the knowledge gained from the experience. Often, it is that people now see the hero's greatness, which earns them admiration back in the ordinary world. For Dorothy and friends, it's the knowledge that what they thought was missing was inside them all along.

10. **The road back:** The road back is the consequence of conquering the central ordeal. The hero may be pursued by the enemy's henchmen, who may be after that reward. The hero decides that at this point it is time to return to the ordinary

world. In *Jaws*, the two survivors, still in the dangerous water, paddle their way to safety.

11. **Resurrection:** The hero is challenged once again, and we get to see how much they have changed. We will only know if the hero really learned from the ordeal by having them face one last challenge. Neo, killed by Agent Smith, is resurrected once Trinity declares her love for him.

12. **Return with elixir:** The journey is meaningless unless the hero brings back some token, elixir, or treasure. It's often simply the change, or a symbol of the change, that the experience facilitated.

That is a lot to fit in a movie, let alone your one-minute story! However, it is certainly a winning formula that has been used for countless films and books. While this type of recipe model may be suited best for fiction, it can also frame your personal stories, especially the ones about overcoming adversity. I admit that it may be challenging, but this frame can enhance any story.

Here is the list pared down to make it more manageable. As a challenge, consider a story that you often tell about overcoming a problem and see whether it fits this modified model:

1. Ordinary world (what the world is like now, before the ordeal)
2. Call to adventure (what prompted the need to face the ordeal)
3. Refusal of the call (the hero's resistance to having to face the ordeal)
4. Crossing the threshold (acceptance of the call to take action, from which point there is no turning back)
5. Tests (the challenges the hero endures along the way to facing the ordeal)
6. Approach to the inmost cave (after the challenges, it is the journey to the showdown)
7. Central ordeal (the showdown)
8. Reward (what the hero learned from the journey)
9. Return with elixir (how the hero changed).

The hero's journey at its core is a story about an ordinary person who wants something, and the trials they must go through to get it. Why they want it and how they get it is the content of the story. The journey plays such a dominate role in modern storytelling in part because change is a fundamental element of the journey—that change is what is needed for the character to get what they want, even if it is only to survive. It also mirrors the journeys we often face in real life.

Building Blocks Model: The Story Spine

Like recipe models, building blocks models provide a structure that flows in a specific order, but are far less prescriptive about what each element looks like. A popular building blocks model is the story spine, which is recommended as a way to structure true stories.

The story spine model is structured as follows:

- Once upon a time . . .
- Every day . . .
- But, one day . . .
- Because of that . . .
- Because of that . . .
- Until, finally . . .
- And, ever since then . . .

The story spine provides structure, but does not suggest the type of content that should go into each block. However, most models follow a pattern similar to the hero's journey—the beginning of the story in the ordinary world, followed by the moment when everything changed, and ending in a new world.

The words at the beginning of each line are prompts, and are not used in the story itself. Here is an example of a story I wrote using the prompts:

- Once upon a time . . . I was a technical support representative, and I worked on a team with about 10 peers.
- Every day . . . We had lunch together and often hung out after work and on the weekends.
- But, one day . . . Our manager got promoted and his position became available. Everyone wanted to apply for it, but we were

afraid to talk about it for fear that the competition would disrupt our relationships. I applied for it and got the job.

- Because of that . . . I felt like everyone had turned on me. I was busier so couldn't hang out as much, but they were also meeting up without inviting me. They were still friendly to me in the office, but there was a distance that was beginning to affect my job.
- Because of that . . . My manager reprimanded me for being too concerned about whether people liked me and not focusing on the call center numbers. He told me he promoted me because I was already a leader and that I needed to get back what I lost.
- Until, finally . . . I decided to tackle my insecurities head-on. I met with the team and they told me that they thought I had changed. I told them that I thought they had changed. We talked through our differences and re-established expectations.
- And, ever since then . . . I was more comfortable in my managerial role, and we all realized that our friendship didn't go away. It just evolved.

The story spine reinforces the idea that in a good story, something happens. Events are occurring that move the story along, and each event builds on its predecessor. The model encourages the storyteller to communicate a sequence of events that culminate in a change. The pattern is not "this happened" and "this happened." It's "this happened," and consequently "this happened," and so on. There is a rhythm, a momentum driving the story forward and taking the listener with it.

Building Blocks Model: ICAP

All stories have a structure. The question is whether the structure you are using is serving your intent. When I am facilitating, many of my stories are not planned, so it is a challenge for me to structure and frame them. I can prepare for weeks, but once I am in front of people, my only goal is to remember the next part of the plot. Remembering that my story should fall into a nine-step formula is unlikely. I recommend assessing your own needs while drawing on the models that have stood the test of time for inspiration.

Any model I use should be simple enough to use spontaneously. The model I use now is one I constructed, and like the other models introduced here, it is influenced by the models that came before it. It includes four elements: intent, context, action, and point—ICAP.

Intent: What Do I Want the Story to Do?

Intent is the first consideration because it influences the entire story. It answers the question, "What do I want this story to do?" It works like a trigger. An event occurs that alerts me that I need a story to fulfill a specific purpose. The trigger could be preplanned and embedded in the content or caused by a participant's comment or some other interaction.

For example, I told a story in chapter 1 about my manager suggesting that I stop sending emails at night to my direct reports because they may think that I want a response that same evening. That story is part of my cache of stories because it's simple, short, and can be used as an example of unintended consequences or of managers modeling the behavior they want to see in their team. If I'm teaching a class for new managers and we are discussing either of those behaviors, I may plan to use that story—or it may simply pop into my head. Further, I have options for which perspective I want to tell the story from. I could either tell it from the employees' point of view to promote empathy, or I could tell it from the manager's point of view if I want learners to visualize that situation. What I choose depends on my intent, which is driven by what I think it will contribute to the conversation.

There is a difference between intent and point, which falls at the end of my model. I can begin my story with an intent in mind, but I believe that once a story comes out of my mouth, it no longer belongs to me. Listeners will take what they hear, coat it in the context of their own experiences, and derive meaning from what comes out on the other side.

Context: Where Am I Taking Them?

The process begins with intent, but I do not announce the intent to the learners. Story construction begins with this second element, context. Every story lives somewhere. That place is defined by time, location, perspective, the people involved, and your intent. Context answers the question, "Where am I taking them?" because when I start telling a story, I'm saying, "Come join me on a journey to this other place." Adding these details to the story orients the listener to the foreign world you're inviting them into.

Let's go back to the night emails story. I mentioned that I was not fond of my manager. While it does not show me in the best light, as I've said earlier, to get to a story you have to follow the truth. How would the story have changed had I left out that detail? Then it would have just been my manager giving me some advice, which I would have no reason to question. But that isn't the story, and it does not fit or serve my intent. The story was about my reluctance to change, which in part was because of my relationship with my manager.

While shaping a story's context, be careful to avoid "detail derail." Certain story elements seem more prone to derailment than others. A popular culprit is believing that you need to describe a detailed, proprietary work function for the listener to understand the story. For example, while the story may ultimately be about some feedback your manager gave you about how you were handling a process, you think you need to explain the full process to the listener:

> My manager gave me some less than helpful feedback once. We take in calls through a routing system. My phone lights up when the calls come, but that's only if I'm on available. This is different from the old system where as soon as you hung up, you were automatically made available. We started using the new system because employees didn't have time to add information about the calls to the CRM. So this new system. . . .

If the point of the story is the feedback, just include that there was a breakdown in the call routing process and you were blamed for it. The version of telephone technology you were using is irrelevant because that's not your intent. Your intent is to communicate your frustration with a manager.

People also often get stuck on either sequencing or an environmental aspect of the story. I had a co-worker who told great stories, but she would always get stuck. This is an exaggerated version, but this is what it sounded like to me:

> Remember when I told you—wait, was that you? Did I tell you what my manager said about—no that wasn't you. OK, so my manager told me last week. . . . Wait. Was it last week? When was I out?

Details do matter, but while context is detail, detail is not always context. Remember that your context serves your intent—but do not strangle the life out of it.

Decisions for what to reveal and what to hold back are influenced by your intent, but there is another crucial question that you must answer: Whose story is this? This question is not as easy to answer as you may think. Should the focus be on my experience, or the experience of someone else in the story? It's true that every story I tell reflects my experience. Events will be described as I saw them and statements will be interpreted as I understood them. I'm even determining what the listener should know. In a sense, the story will always be mine, but that doesn't mean I'm the focus. The person who is the focus has the problem and the agency to fix it. The focus is on the one who goes through the transformation. That's what's wonderful about a rich and complex story. You can repurpose it repeatedly, changing the focus to suit your needs. This only works if you are intentional about it and know what to add and remove when shaping the context.

Action: What Are the Leading, Key, and Consequential Events?

Action is the motor that powers your story. How well you manage each event can make or break the experience you're creating for the learner. Remember, you're not telling us what happened, you're telling us a story. We talked about events and event types in chapter 1, but action takes your events a step further. An event is what happened, but I think of action as how I describe how it happened. There's one rule: Make us see it.

Our focus here is on stories that are to be spoken, not read. In part 3, we will talk about delivery because you'll be expected to act out your stories whenever possible. Instead of telling us what someone said to you, become that person and say it to us. We want to be there and empathize with what you felt. So, throughout part 2 as we talk about what to include in your stories, think about the events you're including and how you can bring them to life—literally.

One way to ensure that you can bring the action to life is tell the story in a way that gives your characters agency. Present events as something the people in your story did, caused, or reacted to, rather than making them a constant victim of circumstance. Your learners are more likely to identify with people who seem in control of their lives because adults want to be seen as being in control of their own.

Often, it is as simple as using active rather than passive language. Other times it may be more complicated because of your perception of the events. But stories that are intended to teach are dead in the water if the protagonist is presented as someone who is helpless. If your goal is to influence behavior changes, the targeted behavior needs to be in the story.

Point: How Will Learners Gain From This Story?

You may have an intent in mind, but once you tell a story, it no longer belongs to you. The "point," or the moral of the story, is for the learner to decipher, not for the facilitator to dictate. We facilitate the process of learners arriving at what they believe to be the point. Perhaps a shared meaning can grow from that discussion, but that's not necessarily the goal. Learners should construct their own meaning and then have that perspective corroborated, disrupted, or challenged by the rest of the class. True learning happens when people can apply knowledge and skills to different contexts. Facilitating "point construction" contributes to that.

When I was new to training, I didn't embrace this philosophy. If I had a story that I believed made a specific point, that was the point of the story. It was not open for interpretation. *My* point had a purpose. Sometimes the point was logistical, perhaps to serve as transitions between topics. If the learners started offering alternative readings of my story, I would have to honor those readings and still somehow navigate back to my intended point to make the transition. This circle back was easier if the points the learners made were off base. But, usually, their points were better than mine!

To avoid all this, I had to learn to let go of my belief that the story-teller owns the meaning, and let the story do what it is supposed to do: Provoke thought. Listeners are supposed to pull from the context of their lives and make the story their own. Has someone ever told you a story and repeated it if you interpreted a different meaning than the story-teller's intent, as if you either didn't understand the story or the person didn't "tell it right"? No, you understood the story just like the learners understood me. But they are not me. I'm telling my story, but the listener is taking in a different story—it is the story of them experiencing my story and how it connects to their lives. How could I possibly presume that we will all arrive at the same place at the same time? That "place" is the point. Now, I am prepared for the possibility of my transition not being as elegant as I planned, but that messiness can be the best part of teaching and learning.

Using the ICAP or any model is the easy part. It only takes care of the logistics. If you only told a story using ICAP or any other directive model, it may be effective, but you wouldn't be using storytelling to its fullest potential. The question is, what are the qualities of a good story? Which types of stories are good for teaching and learning? Which stories connect with learners? Let's find out in part 2.

Wrap-Up: Structure Is Everything

You can shape stories using two types of story models. Recipe models provide a framework for events in a set sequence. Building blocks models focus more on specific types of content layered together, with each component building off the one that came before it.

The hero's journey is an example of the recipe model. It is a popular framework for stories that focus on the protagonist's transformation from ordinary person to hero. The story spine is an example of a building blocks model. It does not specify what type of content you should use; instead, it provides prompts that encourage you to focus on the events that propel your story forward.

The ICAP model, which is the model I use, is a building blocks model that consists of very broad buckets of information that you gather by examining what you want the story to accomplish.

PART 2

Selecting and Shaping Stories That Teach

t sounds so simple. Just tell stories while you facilitate. You have experience, right? You have led and followed, won and lost, spoken up and shut up—and someone trusted you to lead a group of participants through a course, so surely your insights have some utility. You just have to take those experiences and say them out loud. And, bam! You're a storyteller! I am being sarcastic, of course.

Facilitating with stories is not simple, especially if you assume the process begins with facilitating with stories. It does not. It starts long before the moment when you are facing a group of 20 managers—maybe two minutes before, maybe 50 years before. It starts with living, experiencing, reflecting, and most of all, sense-making; that is, looking for the universal meaning in what happened to you.

The work does not end there. The challenge of identifying and selecting stories that fit the context and your intent, often on a moment's notice, lies ahead. It is best to have a cache of curated and vetted stories that you can draw from. But what types of stories should you add to your cache? Do stories that work well as facilitation tools have specific qualities? In part 2, we will look at what types of stories help facilitate learning: stories that connect, show change, are relevant, and entertain.

4

Stories That Connect

ob loved operating gas stations. He loved the work, the people, and even the smell of gasoline in the morning. After decades in the field, he traded his store keys for a training manual. When I met him, he had spent the last five years helping to create a new generation of managers who loved the job as much as he did. When you saw him teach, it was clear that he was highly regarded for his experience; but most of all, the learners loved him. These "oil guys and gals," seasoned and often cynical (or realistic, as they would say), looked at him with childlike admiration as they hung on his every word. They were not an easy bunch to get any reaction from, let alone a positive one. They were field operations folks with little desire to spend eight hours in a hotel conference room learning about the job they had been doing for years.

I first saw Bob teach when he was facilitating a course I was redesigning. We were in a cramped, windowless hotel conference room in downtown Chicago. The learners were experienced and vocal about what they liked and, mostly, what they didn't like. While most of his stories were relevant and business focused, several seemed so random or intensely personal that I struggled to find their purpose or his intent in telling them. But as the participants shared knowing glances and nods with Bob and with one another, it was clear that while I may have been confused, they were not.

The second time I saw him teach was in an airy, bright, beige hotel conference room near O'Hare Airport. This time around, the crowd was younger and less experienced. While he was teaching the same material, he told fewer stories, and the ones he did tell were different or altered from the last time I'd heard them. They were less personal, and more focused on tangible outcomes. Most of all, they were less, well, scary. The downtown playlist consisted of spontaneous fires, constant employee theft, and brazen robberies. The suburban playlist was limited to defiant employees, discourteous customers, and disfigured product displays.

I asked him if he believed his facilitation style changed based on the audience. He said, "Of course." I asked him in which ways. "All of them," he said. "The material won't connect otherwise."

The material won't connect otherwise.

He had a bank of stories in his head that he learned to swap in and out of rotation depending on the audience. For him, stories are tools and storytelling is the strategy for how to use them most effectively. His goal wasn't just to teach, but to connect.

Why Connection Matters in Stories

Stories can help facilitate connections among ideas and people. Bob used his stories to connect theoretical content to the manager's role, and then connect those theories to how to do the job in real life. Because of that experience, he could empathize with participants and tell stories in which they could recognize themselves, consequently connecting his experience and theirs. His stories made them feel seen, heard, and validated. They saw themselves in Bob, and he knew connections were helpful to the learning process.

Connections bridge a starting point and a destination, and at a basic level, this is what facilitation is all about—building bridges and helping guide people across them. Most narratives serve that function by giving us insight into times and places far from our own. You are not a Danish prince who lived during the late middle ages, yet somehow you can probably relate to Hamlet's internal war between loyalty and conscience. Narratives intended for learning do the same thing—they make content, people, and concept relatable. That relationship is the connection and, if reinforced with learning principles, it facilitates learning.

Stories That Feature Connections

Knowing how to identify the connective elements in stories is critical to being able to select stories that bridge a gap. I find that the connective elements are usually near the parts of the story where you can let the learners in. For example, when Bob talked about managing employees he had never worked with before (perhaps they worked on a different shift), he would stop talking about his experience and ask the group whether they had the same experience and to share their thoughts. Select stories with areas where it is possible to break the "fourth wall," that imaginary barrier standing between the storyteller and the listener.

Let's discuss the types of stories facilitators can use to form connections:

- stories that bridge the course to reality
- stories that link the old and the new
- stories that create empathy.

The Real Deal: Bridging the Course to Reality

Theories are useful for guiding people through a variety of similar and even dissimilar situations. However, they can also be frustrating because it is not always clear how theories that look good on paper will play in real life. When we use stories, we can bring those theories to life and connect them to our day-to-day experiences.

"Where Is Everybody?" was the title of the first aired episode of *The Twilight Zone*. A man with no memory of who he is or where he came from finds himself alone in a deserted town. He wanders around looking for people or answers until he eventually cracks under the strain. We discover that it was all in his head. In reality, it was an air force training exercise intended to test how much loneliness astronauts could endure. What better way to bridge the gap between reality and theory than to encourage people to live out that theory in real life?

Every so often, I get to tell an interactive story where I can intersperse real events with real-time feedback from the learners while simultaneously teaching theory. For example, I have a story I tell whenever I'm teaching a management course about how I once had a manager who gave us inside information about impending layoffs. I don't know what our company policy was, but it's safe to assume that telling your employees about layoffs weeks before the company announces them is discouraged. As I describe the questionable decisions my manager made, I stop and present the group with "what if" scenarios that are couched in basic theories of managerial ethics: Would you tell your team about the layoffs? If you knew that your team members were not going to lose their jobs, but nearly everyone one else was, would that change your answer?

We all have theories that are based on personal experience. But, we often see these theories as irrefutable truths that qualify as common sense and with which everyone else should agree. I often select stories that put these "common sense" theories to the test to see how they hold up. These types of stories are often intended to disconnect learners from existing theories and then expand their thinking on new ones, as presented in the content.

I was once teaching a group of new supervisors about the nuances of motivation. It is an important concept that is easy to understand, but in practice motivating people remains difficult. The new supervisors in my class were stuck on grand gestures, the grandest of all being money. They believed that saying "good job" only went so far, and would not lead to sustained motivation. While that is often true, I knew from personal experience how something that seems like a small gesture to the giver can have a significant impact on the receiver. So, I told them a story:

> My first job after college was in a technical support call
> center. Once, I was preparing to attend a meeting where I
> knew that management was going to inform us that we were
> bad at our jobs. We were too slow to answer and too quick
> to escalate the call to a higher level rather than manage
> the call ourselves. It was hard to stay motivated when, as
> a senior employee, I was the one taking all the escalations

while still making my own call quotas. I was unhappy and unmotivated and got through each day by thinking about one call at a time and never beyond that. I couldn't hide my frustration with management and the fact that they used reprimands instead of timely feedback and training to improve job performance. My plan for this meeting was to make a stink and ask questions that they didn't want to answer.

I arrived at the conference room first so that I could select a power seat. Soon after, the company president walked in. We were both in our late 20s, and back then I was surprised to work for a company whose president was so young. I had never spoken to him and I wasn't sure he knew I existed. We were alone in the conference room and I just folded my arms and looked away.

After a few seconds of silence, he walked around the table, looked me in the eye, and said, "We've never met before. But I hear you on the phone when I pass by your cubicle every day. I know that if I called into support and you got the call, I would be in good hands." Huh? It was an unsolicited compliment that seemed to serve no purpose other than to communicate his admiration for my work. He appealed to my ego, so of course I was happy. But there was something else.

He was shy and reticent, and when he said he walked by my cube every day, he was right. He walked past the entire department without stopping or looking at any of us. We were long resigned to the fact that we were invisible to him.

I could tell as he spoke that he was nervous and in unfamiliar territory. He took a personal risk not only by complimenting me, but by speaking to me at all. I felt both appreciated. Later, after reflection, I understood that my job was bigger than those calls. My work had an impact on everyone in the company and on every customer I talked to. For me, acknowledging that was a risk. And if the CEO was willing to take one, so was I.

That was many, many years and jobs ago, and it still is the best compliment I ever received. Small things can motivate people and, for me, the key was that his comment felt genuine and unrehearsed. That mattered more to me than what he actually said. When I use this story, I want the participants to challenge their current way of thinking and connect to an expanded theory of how to motivate performance.

Linking the Old and the New

Instructional designers often leverage existing beliefs to help participants master new ideas. When teaching a new system, a facilitator may include examples from how an older process was used to help participants learn the new processes. We can use stories the same way by telling ones that tie old beliefs to new ones.

Consider the new supervisors I used to train at the bank. Many of them were promoted into the job because they were good at the job they had previously. The promotion was more of a reward for good work than a strategic move on behalf of the bank's leadership. Consequently, to many of these new managers, the idea of a "good job" was tied to their old one. If they did not roll their sleeves up and get down in the trenches with their team, they believed they were doing a bad job. My goal as a facilitator was to help them see that managing means getting work done through others. Management is a different job than what they had been doing, so the expectations were different. You still have to get down in the trenches, just not the same trenches as before.

I recall telling one class about Kim, a co-worker I had several years before who worked long hours and produced great work.

> When a management position came up, Kim was the logical choice for a promotion. She was dedicated to her job and one of the best designers in the department. She accepted the promotion and saw it as a reward and a validation of her head-down strategy. Then, she went back to business as usual, humbly reminding us that she was still the same person. Nothing had changed. Except it had—everything had changed, whether she liked it or not.

Her employees wanted Kim to lead. They asked her questions and tried to show her their work. However, her response was to tell the other designers what she would do in their situation or, sometimes, even taking the project over herself in an effort to "save her team." She was just doing everything she did as an individual contributor. She considered management tasks an unnecessary distraction from her real job, which, to her, was still working as a designer.

After about six months, she asked to be placed back in her old position and promote someone else instead. Companies don't quite work like that, so she was either going to have to adapt or leave the company and find her "old job" somewhere else. She chose to leave.

Why did this happen? Neither she, nor her manager, who should have supported her transition to manager, seemed to recognize that while Kim had a new job, she was still doing the old one. It was disheartening for Kim to think that she was not doing a good job, especially when all the praise she had enjoyed until then turned into criticism. If she wanted to do a good job now, she had to focus on being a better leader, not a better designer.

I selected this story because I knew that participants would recognize themselves in Kim and not want to meet the same fate. Focusing on the fact that their jobs had changed wasn't enough to convince participants that a change was needed. I had to change my focus from the job itself to the learners and their identities. If I wanted to connect the driving force behind their old identities to their new ones, I would have to go deeper and tap into the pride they took in being known for doing good work.

Creating Empathy

Empathy is a powerful tool. Volumes have been written about the role of empathy in all aspects of life; however, simply asking people to see a situation from a different point of view does not always work. Storytelling helps us connect participants to new situations from which they may get a small glimpse of other people's lives. Learning often requires a shift in perspective, and encouraging empathy is a proven way to facilitate that change.

During an icebreaker for the supervisory course I facilitated, I asked participants for an analogy to describe management. Most used "babysitting." I suspect it was a bit of groupthink that led them to use that word because although the group started off with descriptions like "rollercoaster" and "football coach," as soon as one person said "babysitting" and the group heard the laugh, nearly everyone used it after that.

Regardless of their motivations, there was clearly some sentiment that management was tantamount to herding children who either could not or would not behave as they were told. I had to remind them that if that was how they truly felt, they were not fooling their employees into thinking that they thought otherwise. I could have simply asked the group how they would feel coming into work every day knowing that their manager thought they were children who needed to be watched. But, while that may resonate with some, telling a story where a protagonist is put in someone else's shoes and sees the world from a different point of view may do a better job of driving the point home.

What was most interesting about these managers was that their perspectives changed so quickly after taking on their new roles. They were individual contributors only a few months before and now were first-level supervisors, which meant that they still had a mountain of hierarchy above them. It may be more effective to help them take a closer look at their current position and relationship to their own managers and to tell their own stories, too. Sometimes, building empathy can come from taking an honest look at your own life rather than someone else's.

Checklist for Selecting Stories That Feature Connections

As you consider which stories to use, ask yourself, does your story:
- ✓ Make connections between the content and real-life experience?
- ✓ Help learners link existing ideas to new ones?
- ✓ Encourage learners to connect their own experiences and ultimately see the world from a different point of view?

Wrap-Up: Forming Connections

Connective elements in stories are essential to great storytelling and facilitating performance. You can use stories to help form a variety of connections: Connect content to real life, connect existing content to new ideas, and connect people's experiences to those of others. The key to using story to facilitate the connections necessary to achieve a performance is to build bridges and help people cross them.

5

Stories That
Show Change

arly in my training career, I was assigned to design and
teach a course on sensitivity. However, I was unsettled by
the prospect of doing so. While our basic, corporate curriculum consisted of professional development courses—or
what are commonly referred to as soft-skill courses (a label
I reject; there is nothing "soft" about interpersonal skills)—customized
requests for training were usually on technical topics or content intended
to support new initiatives. I didn't know what prompted the request, but
I did know that training could support an implemented solution—not be
the solution itself. I hoped they knew that too.

I met with the manager who made the request. I was still new to
training needs assessments, but managed to get him to tell me what
happened. He said it all started with an investigation into alleged drug
abuse and distribution on the premises and ended with proof of wide-
spread intimidation among the call center employees. His solution: Fire
only those whose actions were so egregious that they were currently in
police custody, and put the rest through a one-hour sensitivity training
course. All training sessions were to be delivered in one day. And this plan

was supposed to create a change in these employees that would last a lifetime. . . . I was not as optimistic as the manager.

I knew I could change nothing in an hour, so instead I decided to create a modest goal that my manager and the call-center manager could agree on. I had not even heard of learning objectives yet, but I was experienced enough to know that the best I could hope for given my constraints was to get participants to agree on what harassment looks like. I wrote a few case studies, emailed them in a document to participants, and asked them to complete an online survey indicating whether each situation constituted harassment and why or why not. Throughout the week prior to the course, as I watched the slices of my survey results pie chart grow and shrink in unexpected ways, I started to worry about how the course was going to play out.

When training day arrived, I did not know what to expect. The survey results were anonymous, but once the people who held opinions that were not so politically correct learned that they were in the majority, they were emboldened to say exactly what they felt during our session. While open and honest conversation was the point of the class, I had not anticipated that much honesty. Fifteen minutes in, we were nowhere near the one objective I had—recognition. The truth is, I did not give much thought to how I was going to persuade them to change their personal definitions of harassment. In my naiveté and professional inexperience, I expected the majority of people to recognize harassment, and I thought the few who did not would see how unpopular their opinions were and then be open to learning something new. I was wrong.

I needed to tap into something I did not have access to—their intrinsic motivation to change. I knew that this would take more than data about the benefits of diversity and reductive stories about hurt feelings. Storytelling may be a good way to handle this, but what type of story would you tell in this situation? We have talked about how a change is essential to all stories. But in situations when the change is the performance goal, the story about the change could also be instructive. It must both describe a change (as all stories should do) and encourage a change in the listener— ideally it would also demonstrate how to go about making the change. This chapter is about the qualities a story should have so that the change you are facilitating taps into the person's intrinsic motivation to make the change.

Why Change Matters in Stories

The most effective stories describe a change. We are talking about stories that have utility beyond memories and anecdotes. Stories used to facilitate learning are in the same category as meaningful books and films (which also focus on transformation) because, just like stories intended for those media, these stories are used as tools to present and reinforce specific narratives in service of encouraging a change in perception or behavior.

When I was in graduate school for writing, our instructors frequently gave us feedback on our stories by asking, "Why are you telling us this?" We knew to interpret their feedback as a request to make the case for a story's existence within the story itself. In other words, they didn't want us to tell them why we wrote it. They wanted us to strengthen the story so that readers felt like they were experiencing something consequential. Our story had to matter so much to someone that it needed to be not just told, but remembered. As Blake Snyder (2005) wrote in his book, *Save the Cat! The Last Book on Screenwriting You'll Ever Need,* "I think the reason that characters must change . . . is because if your story is worth telling, it must be vitally important to everyone involved." And for something to matter, there must be something at stake—something that can be lost or won. Change, causing it or avoiding it, raises the stakes every time.

Stories That Feature Change

You need stories that feature a change, but change in what way? There are three qualities to look for:

- stories that motivate participants to make a change
- stories that feature a change that required agency
- stories that show both a change and how to make that change.

Motivation: Why Make the Change?

I had one goal for that sensitivity training class: I wanted everyone who went through the session to agree on what constituted harassment. The plan was to have participants read the policy (that, in part, defined harassment as unwanted behavior perceived as intimidating or threatening), read a scenario that describes a workplace incident, and then answer questions on how consistent the events in the scenario were with the policy.

I remember only one of the scenarios. It stands out because we had such a heated discussion about it. The scenario described the behavior of an employee, John, who was a 60-year-old man with about 30 years on the job. He was a "hugger," who wrapped his arms around everyone he met. He had been doing it for so long without consequence that he did not bother to consider whether people wanted to be touched. He figured everyone could use a hug. As far as anyone knew, no one had ever complained to management or HR.

When a new female employee, Karen, is introduced to John on her first day, he moves in for a hug. She backs away, but he moves forward and hugs her anyway. Karen is horrified and embarrassed. During the next three months, he attempts to hug her several more times, with varying levels of success. Finally, she goes to human resources and reports him.

In the survey that accompanied the scenario, I asked participants whether they believed John's behavior was consistent with the company's description of harassment. I purposely avoided asking outright whether it was harassment. More than 75 percent of the participants said no, John's behavior was not consistent with the company's definition. When we discussed the survey results during the live session, most argued semantics or wanted a clear description of Karen's behavior. The scenarios were written to allow for a gray area so that the answers would be less obvious. In this case, however, the correct answer was that John's behavior was consistent with the company's definition of harassment. Those who did not see it as problematic would have to be motivated to think otherwise. But how?

Make the Change Look Desirable

People are motivated to change if the result will lead to a positive outcome. Consequently, the story that supports the change should end on a positive note, although you cannot guarantee outcomes, positive or negative.

When I tell stories with positive outcomes, I tend to gloss over the details. Perhaps it is humility that makes me leave out all the hard work and good luck that played a role in bringing about a wonderful opportunity. It sounds like bragging to me. Unfortunately, when you leave out details like this, it makes the good outcome look too easily won, which also sounds like bragging.

I've found that my stories tend to skew negative because I remember the details more clearly and I find them to be more interesting and entertaining. But that penchant does nothing to make an outcome look desirable. Sometimes when I get to the end of a story that I initially intended to end on a positive note, the look on the participants' faces says, "So, is that a good thing?" That is just one of many biases I have, and I am sure you have your own. This is why it is so important to be intentional with the stories you select, instead of just trusting that the story that pops into your head is the appropriate one to tell. Select stories that champion the change your participants want and will motivate them to learn the behaviors needed to make that change happen.

It Is the Journey, Not the Destination

There are no guarantees. Learning how to create the perfect resume may not get you the job. When the destination is far away or uncertain, participants may get discouraged. In those cases, focus on the rewards of the journey instead. Consider the hero's journey and all the action films that use it as a framework. We know the chances of the hero surviving are high. And even if they do not survive, the outcome still skews positive because "they died so others can live." We know this will be the outcome, but we still want to see the journey because that is the point. We want to see the events that facilitated the transformation during the journey. The hero must earn the outcome.

Select stories in which what is gained by each leg of the journey is desirable, for better or worse. A lot of people ask me about freelancing and running my own business, and I have many stories to share. I usually center them on milestones: when I got my first client on my own, when I was able to increase my rates, how I gained my clients' trust, and so forth.

But it was what I learned on the journey that mattered most. For example, when you're an internal employee, your manager determines salary increases based on past work. She has worked with you all year and, in theory, knows your performance and how it stacks up against others on the team. Or, you may simply expect a raise because of the history of performance. It's different when you're a consultant. Once you decide you need to charge more for your services, making that happen can be a long, trial-and-error process, and the results are not guaranteed. When potential clients walk away and you adjust your strategy for the next time around, that is where the learning happens.

Agency: Who or What Makes the Change?

Writers and critics talk a lot about characters having agency, which is the act of exerting power. In storytelling, agency refers to whether a character appears to be charting their own course or is a hapless victim to whom events simply happen. If the character does not have agency at the beginning of the story, we expect them to get it as part of their transformation. There are plenty of good stories where the protagonist has no control, but you have to ask that central question—what do you expect the listener to gain from hearing a story about a person who had no control over their own circumstances?

Adults want to see people in control of their own lives and like to feel that way as well. This fact also influences how adults learn: "Andragogy suggests that adults have a self-concept of being responsible for their own lives and expect others to treat them as being capable of self-direction" (Knowles, Holton, and Swanson 2005). Agency enhances stories that facilitate learning.

Destiny Is in Your Hands—Or Is It?

There is little point in facilitating any performance solution if the target learners don't have the extrinsic power to make the changes needed to adopt the desired behaviors. If no structures or procedures to support the change are in place back on the job, transfer of learning will be crippled. Select stories where the protagonist is able to actually make the changes you are suggesting.

When I attend conferences, I often avoid "case study" sessions where presenters walk us through a successful project they completed for their organizations or for a client. These are usually considered the most practical type of session, because the presenters are sharing how they moved past theory to application. Great, but I am always more curious about the limitations they faced and the support they received. For many learning and development professionals, lack of organizational support and resources are greater limitations than their own individual skill.

Once, when I was still an employee, I attended a conference breakout session about making great videos for an e-learning course. This was back when company communications were still fueled by BlackBerries, so no one was yet walking around with production studio equipment in their pocket. The presenters had great stories about their storyboarding processes and production challenges. The problem was that, according to them, all you needed to make "good" video was a room with a green screen and multimedia equipment. Most of the audience just glanced at each other with a look that said, "What?" My company was in absolutely no position to provide any of that. Of course, I never asked either—but when you have to bargain for a software upgrade, the possibility of getting a green screen and equipment seems unlikely.

You Can Do It!

If participants do not believe they can make the change because of real or imagined personal barriers, they may not adopt the new performances. Learners must have enough self-efficacy to believe that the desired performance is achievable. Think of the quote attributed to Henry Ford: "Whether you think you can, or you think you can't—you're right."

One company I worked for had a professional development course about identifying and living out your dreams. We went through exercises that helped us visualize what we wanted to do with our lives and then create a plan to get there. I thought it was an odd addition to the corporate curriculum, and I thought it was odder still after I took the course myself. If it actually met its performance objectives, most people would quit their jobs within six months of taking the course—unless you were already where you wanted to be.

Years later, I can see how the course was useful, although most of us were staying put. I was being too literal. The actionable lesson was discovering all the tools we could use to facilitate turning our goals into reality. This skill is applicable to both our dreams and our realities. The instructor mostly told stories about people who, as they say, grew where they were planted. He talked about how if we were clear about what we wanted, we could start taking steps toward that distant goal today from where we are now.

Make the Change or It Will Be Made for You

The threat of having your agency compromised by someone or something else can be a great motivator. There are times when the performance you are looking for requires a lunging rather than a leaning in toward a change. The time for ruminating and considering options may be ending. In these cases, select stories about when a threat is visible and swiftly moving toward the protagonist, but they acted when it was needed.

You may think the word *threat* is too negative and want to replace it with a softer word, like *encourage*. I would not. Subtlety is not a viable option if you want to have the desired impact. At their core, these stories are about a potentially aggressive resolution to what may have been a prolonged period of passive or passive-aggressive behavior. In other words, the story focuses on an undesirable situation created by the protagonist's action or inaction, and they must take action—right now—or face even more undesirable consequences. Select stories where the protagonist sat safely in the ordinary world, received the call to adventure, and refused the call over and over again until they had no choice but to cross the threshold into the special world.

Instructions for How to Change

Refusing the call of change is not always a matter of agency. People often do not know how to change. For example, I told a story in chapter 4 about employees who were frequently promoted to management based on their ability to do their current job well. The assumption is that if you can do a job well, you must be able and qualified to supervise people doing that job. The new supervisor is often simply dropped into the role with no management training. In some cases, like in retail jobs, there may be no superior or peer to coach the supervisor. So, it's up to the new supervisor to realize that the new job requires a new set of skills. Meanwhile, upper management is very specific about what performance targets the supervisor needs to hit. But, how?

When I facilitate courses for employees who need to learn a skill that may be new to them, I make my stories more specific. These learners often don't have patience for theory and nuance. After describing a change the protagonist made, hands immediately shoot up followed by different variations of how, why, when, where, and what. Let's look at some types of stories that can provide this level of detail.

Old Dog, New Tricks

Let's think about a scenario: After working through a process the same way for a long time, you are asked to make a change. You may wonder if it's possible to learn a new way of doing something. Or is it too late to change? Throughout the late 1990s and early 2000s, there was an uptick in companies either upgrading from old mainframe systems or using technology to automate procedures for the first time. Many of my technical training assignments centered on teaching people how to use new software to complete tasks they had completed manually for years. It was a challenge because you are navigating participants' feeling about the change while teaching software and, often, the basics of how to use a computer.

In chapter 2, I described the "Z" format, a feature-based approach to technical training, and contrasted it with training that focuses on the more practical knowledge needed to complete whole tasks. I used stories to provide context, explain what they needed to accomplish, and then give instructions. This is another one of those cases where specificity is vital, especially for analytical professions that tend to attract people who are literal in their approach to understanding.

It Was Inside You All Along

Sometimes I use stories to explain how a methodology or process is more complicated than it seems on the surface. I introduce the variable considerations required to make a fully informed decision. I also use stories to do the opposite, that is, attempt to make a complicated task look easy. One of the keys to making something new seem easy is to tie it to what the learner is already doing. Focus on how they can use the same approach they have always used, but now using a new tool instead of doing it manually.

A story strategy can help participants feel as though little is changing. "Before and after" stories work well for this. You talk—or better yet, encourage them to talk—about how the previous approach worked, and then tell the same story, replacing the process steps with the new ones. However, this approach only works if you are being honest. It is not helpful to pretend that a complicated task is easy. Don't label the task as "difficult" or "easy"; simply let the story speak for itself.

Checklist for Selecting Stories That Feature Change

As you consider which stories to use, ask yourself, does your story:
- ✓ Provide examples of positive outcomes so that learners are motivated to make the change?
- ✓ Help ensure that learners understand that making the change is within their power?
- ✓ Give guidance on how to make the change?

Wrap-Up: Nothing Stays the Same

It is important for story protagonists to experience a transformation, which is usually the purpose of the story. If the protagonist's change mirrors the change in performance you are seeking from the participants, then the story should tap into their intrinsic motivation.

Stories can facilitate motivation by making the change seem desirable, ensuring that participants can make the change, and, at least at a high level, explaining within the context of the story how to actually make the transformations. It is also easier to believe that change is possible if you take the focus off the destination and put it on the rewards of the journey instead.

6

Stories That Are Relevant

ccording to adult learning theory, learners are self-directed and motivated to seek out knowledge when they need it. That motivation can be extrinsic or intrinsic, and it's intrinsic motivation that brings "aspirational registrants" to my classes. They come because they believe they'll need a specific skill set in the future. Maybe. This happens a lot in the public registration courses I teach. While participants who are overqualified for the course show up, it's far more common to have participants who have no experience using Microsoft Excel, but who register for an advanced Microsoft Excel course because it fits their schedule. Teaching to different levels simultaneously is part of the job and to be expected, but it makes telling relevant stories a challenge.

Once I was teaching a course called Strategic Decision Making for Managers. It was an advanced, internal course, and while registration was open to anyone in the company, I did not expect to see any aspirational registrants that day. As we went around the room giving our experience, one participant, Jesse, said that this was his third day.

"Welcome, Jesse. What management experience do you have from your previous employer?"

"No," he said. "This is my third day on any job. I just graduated back in June."

"And you are a manager now? Did your manager encourage you to take the class?"

"No to both. I just thought it would be interesting."

I later learned there were several other people who had never managed in the class. It came down to a 50-50 split. I began to wonder whether this could still qualify as a management class just because the content was at that level. I could not ignore the needs of either side of the management divide. I knew I had to teach the content as-is, but the challenge would be to make it relevant to people at so many levels, especially for a level that the class is not designed for.

As I facilitated the course and participants answered questions about what to do in certain management situations, I noticed a subtle divide emerging. A manager would give a classic "management" answer to a question, and then a nonmanager would challenge that answer from the employee point of view. For example, one section of the course focused on selecting employees for promotion. We used an example of two employees—one was new to the company with fresh insights and an MBA, and the other was a long-time employee who had already taken on some management responsibilities. The managers stressed that the decision should be based on what was best for the company and the department, while some nonmanagers believed that loyalty to the existing employee should be the primary concern. Before we could hash out the best answer, the strategy-versus-loyalty debate hijacked the conversation.

I liked that the managers were reminded about the employee perspective, but it became more of a distraction than a benefit. I needed to change the conversation and get the nonmanagers to realize what was at stake. I needed a story. But, it could not be one that was only relevant to managers, like the ones we discussed throughout the day. It had to focus on the transition from employee thinking to management thinking. And at the same time, it could not alienate either group. It had to be very narrow in relevance and yet have broad appeal.

Why Relevance Matters in Stories

Relevance has many layers, and it's easy to misjudge what is and is not relevant. Does your story have to be relevant to the content, the learners, or the context? Does it have to be relevant now, or will it only be applicable to the future?

Relevance has always been important, but before we lived in this very customized world, the onus was on the listeners to determine the significance of what they were hearing. There were three versions of the evening news and two versions of your hometown newspaper—you picked one that came the closest to what you believed and, over time, your ideas reflected their commentary. You did the heavy lifting. Now that we can pick and choose what messaging we are exposed to—messaging that reflects our own beliefs back to us—more of the responsibility falls to the messenger. I see this play out in the courses I teach. Learners have grown to expect that nearly all the content, and the examples used to explain it, will be precisely relevant to what they do. If what they're learning doesn't reflect their experience, they'll declare it not relevant.

Ultimately, relevance goes back to those fundamental questions: Why are you telling this story? Why are you telling it now? Why are you telling it to me? In other words, they want to know "What's in it for me?" or WIIFM. Listeners are searching for the answers to these questions as you talk, and if the answers aren't obvious you're in danger of tipping the listeners' cognitive load. A person can only take in so much information at a time, and with all the other information you are expecting them to absorb, trying to figure out the point of your story adds an unnecessary burden.

It's challenging to build and deliver a single, simultaneous experience that accounts for the variety of environments our learners come from, but it will be easier for learners to apply what they have learned back on the job if the lesson fits into their work contexts.

Stories That Feature Relevance

Your experiences are a unique mixture of time, place, circumstance, and, of course, you. We all know this, but it's still easy to fall into thinking that our experiences are universal by default. There are too many variables to presume that the stories you crafted based on your experiences will be relatable out of the box. Perhaps the people in the room will recognize themselves in your stories, but I recommend setting that idea aside and instead being intentional about the ideas you are attempting to convey.

There are three qualities to look for as you unearth stories that will hit close to home:

- stories with a clear, core message that speak to a universal truth
- stories where the recognizable relevance makes the story more engaging
- stories that draw out learners' own stories.

Universal Truth: What's True for All of Us

Look for the "universal truth" in your stories, or look for stories with a universal truth in them. A universal truth is a moral that reflects those predictable aspects of human nature that most of us share. Let's look at some story types that may provide relevance based on what's true for most of us.

Like Mother Always Said. . . .

Right before I quit my job and became a freelancer, I talked to a few people who were already working for themselves, and asked them how they got clients. I had my pen and paper ready so I could write down the address to the website they used or the names of the companies they worked with. Their answers were the same across the board:

"Word of mouth."

I didn't want this to be true. Knowing that I would have to depend on others for opportunities was unsettling. Can't I just sign up some-where? Surely, selling my services would be easier than having to network, contribute to communities, and build an online presence. The people who did that were overachievers. I'd just go the standard route, thank you very much. Now, years later, when people ask me how I get clients, I tell them there's only one way: word of mouth. It's true. It was before and it is now.

On the surface, that story is only useful to people looking to start their own business. Internal employees who get more than enough work handed to them wouldn't be interested in the hustle to get clients. But the hustle touches us all in one form or another. It's quite the turning point in a person's career when they realize that promotions aren't rewards for endurance. They (should be) a strategic move by the company to honor and continue to support a recognized, qualified leader who will help the organization meet its goals. But being a "recognized, qualified leader" means that you are a leader and are seen as one by people who know you as well as those who have only heard of you. How did they hear about you?

"Word of mouth."

People need to feel comfortable with the idea of working with you. They can only do that if they know something about you. And it's better if they get that information from someone they trust. Like my mother used to say, "Someone is always watching." It was true then, and it is now—that's the universal truth.

"A Stitch in Time Saves Nine"

Universal truths, whether direct or subtle, are quick ways to reinforce the relevance of the content. Regardless of who is in the story and what they are doing, if there is a nugget of known truth at the core of the story listeners may find the lessons easier to understand and apply to their work lives. The question for the storyteller is whether you explain the adage first, or tell the story and save the adage until the end.

There is an old saying—or universal truth—that "a stitch in time saves nine." Suppose that you are teaching managers about the importance of documenting employee performance and you have a story about a manager who chose not to. There was no issue until he had to make a strong case for dismissing an employee and did not have the documentation to support his decision. The ending here is obvious. Is it useful to tell a long story just to get to that predictable ending?

If the story has nuance or the ending was unexpected, it may be better to begin with the story. Now, let us pretend the same story has a different ending. Suppose the point you want to make is that by not documenting performance you're failing to do your job, whether or not you need to build a case for an employee's dismissal. Learners may not be expecting the story to end with the manager getting fired for having incomplete records.

Who Can Tell Me Why This Matters?

You may think that you need to be a mind reader—that you need to spend your days trying to fully understand the human condition so that you can tell stories that reveal the hidden truths of humankind. How else are you going to tell stories that are relevant to everyone? Well, you could ask them.

Your story should have a purpose, but the point belongs to the listeners. That being said, you could simply tell your story and facilitate a discussion about what the story means to your participants. This technique could lead to a robust discussion about new story interpretations you never dreamed of. You may choose to never reveal what you think the point is, which may be the point. The story is about you, but the experience people are having in that room, on that day, is about them.

Facilitate Learners' Stories: Who Would Like to Testify?

One way to identify a story's relevance is to ask learners how it is relevant to them. Or, let's go a step further and not tell a story at all. I don't mean you should tell a story and then encourage the learners to tell their own. I mean do not tell one at all. What better way to ensure relevance than to have learners speak about their own experiences? Provide a story prompt with a question to ensure that the stories the learners are selecting from their own caches are relevant. But be careful! If you think staying on target with your own stories is difficult, try facilitating while others are telling their stories. My advice here is to make sure you provide the right prompts and guidance along the way. Let's look at a few examples.

Who Would Like to Share What They Learned About. . . ?

Notice that this prompt is specifically asking what was learned about a topic. You're not asking for a long story about an occurrence that the learner has yet to process and learn from. You're also not looking for a single sentence about a random event. You're asking for a story about a situation in which the storyteller learned something.

Remember, there is a storyteller inside us all. While many of us make a concentrated effort to find that storyteller, some do not. So, when you're facilitating a class for the finance team, don't expect everyone to be able to spin a yarn about how they learned how to be a better manager. You will need to find ways to coach them through that.

Back when we talked about story structure, we explored an example called the story spine. It is a series of prompts designed to help the story-teller build a story with momentum:

- Once upon a time . . .
- Every day . . .
- But, one day . . .
- Because of that . . .
- Because of that . . .
- Until, finally . . .
- And, ever since then . . .

You can use similar prompts to help the storyteller move the story along. Keep them focused on the action—what happened in the story. That action and what happened as a result is what you want to get to. If I sense that the storyteller is getting too deep into the weeds, I ask, "What happened next?" You don't want a series of events—the goal is to find out how one action led to another and another and so on.

What Have You Learned. . . ?

This prompt is a compromise between encouraging learners to tell their own stories and facilitating point identification. We have all experienced that sinking feeling when we realize we are telling a story that has no ending. In a panic, you may just awkwardly announce, "That's it," and then, faced with blank stares, struggle to explain the point. Everyone says "Ohhh," smiles at you, and moves on.

While you could move on if a learner tells a story that slightly misses the mark, as the facilitator, you should help the learner salvage the story. Help them "bang on the lid" by asking questions to help construct meaning for their stories:

1. How did you feel about your behavior?
2. How does that differ from previous behavior?

3. Was that a change? Was that change out of character for you? Did it surprise you?
4. What does that say about you as a person?
5. Did you benefit from the change? Did anyone else?

Checklist for Selecting Stories That Are Relevant

As you consider which stories to use, ask yourself:

✓ Does this story have a clear, core message that speaks to a universal truth?
✓ Does this story clearly communicate why it matters?
✓ Does this story encourage learners to tell their own stories?

Wrap-Up: WIIFM, Live and on the Air

There are strategies to ensuring that stories being used as facilitation tools are relevant to listeners. Participants now expect that what they are learning will be immediately usable and that the examples used to explore content will speak to their experiences. Relevance answers those fundamental questions about why you are telling this story, why you are telling it now, and why you are telling it to me.

Stories that are relevant to disparate audiences are usually based on a universal truth and tap into core emotions that we all share, regardless of context. Invite learners to tell you what's relevant about the stories you tell, or encourage them to tell their own stories, with you helping the storyteller draw out the meaning. It's often more efficient and useful.

7

Stories That Entertain

t was 7:57 a.m., and all 20 participants were seated, four to a table. I could hear the rising and falling hum of chatter behind me as I stood at the receptionist's desk, just a few feet outside the classroom door.

"I'm doing everything I can, Hadiya," she said, as she waited on hold with the copy center.

"My workbooks are supposed to be here," I said. "I can't teach without books."

I wasn't sure whether it was true that I couldn't teach without those workbooks, but I did know that it was now 8:05 a.m., and the volume of the chatter from the classroom was no longer robust enough to pass the doorway. This was back in the early 2000s, before everyone could pull out a laptop and do other work to kill time. Email had to wait until they returned to their desktop computers. I had no idea what to do as I entered the room, but the looks on the participants' faces made it clear that something had to start, and it had to start now.

I had to make a choice—I could act like nothing was out of the ordinary and stall by lengthening the first quarter of the course until the books arrived, or I could immediately confess and let them know that we were going to move forward without all the materials. The first option required some creative tap dancing I wasn't sure I was experienced enough to pull off, and the second would leave participants feeling shortchanged.

I chose a third option. I decided to confess that we had no books, but downplay the significance of that fact. And then, something amazing happened—I had time. Free from the regimented course structure enforced by the workbook, I went rogue and made their experiences and stories the primary source of content. It was a revelation, and I soon began to imagine a future in which I never used a workbook again.

Around 10:45 a.m., the receptionist came to the door and waved at me through the window to get my attention. I told the class to take a quick break. As the participants filed out, the receptionist carried in two large boxes and dropped them onto the table in front of me.

"Finally!" I said. "I can't believe they took so long."

"Hadiya, what time did you get here today?" she asked.

I could tell by her tone that while I didn't yet know why my arrival time mattered, it really, really mattered. I also knew that when someone asks what time you arrived, chances are the right answer is earlier rather than later.

"Early—like 7," I said.

I got there at 7:15, which, while not 7:00, is definitely *like* 7.

"Did you stop by your desk first?"

"No. I haven't been to my desk all morning. I—"

"These books were delivered to your desk at 7:00 this morning. They were sitting there this whole time."

She glared at me. We both knew she had spent most of her morning on the phone with the copy center arguing with them over these books on my behalf. All I could think about was how the copy center should have known that the overnight shift person had delivered the books on his way home, and why would anyone bring the books directly to my desk instead of leaving them in the lobby by the classrooms, and how did he know where my desk was, and how was he able to access my desk directly without a key card to get through the door, but fine. The receptionist was far more interested in her wasted morning than discussing the overnight copy person's seemingly ninja-like abilities.

"Um, sorry. It won't happen again. I promise." I smiled.

She turned with a sigh and said with a singsong lilt, "That's OK, Hadi-ya," while waving her hand over her head and walking out of the room. I later learned that a thoughtful copy center employee had indeed left the box by the front door of the training center. A co-worker who actually did arrive at the office at 7 a.m. saw the boxes with my name on the label and decided to help me further by taking the books to my desk. So, my excite-ment over how I was teaching the course for hours that morning was over-shadowed by what I did not do during a 15-minute window earlier that day.

This story has a classic story structure. There are consequential events, stakes, and a change in the protagonist's views. It has a few lessons that I could focus on if I chose to facilitate with it: Put more focus on the learners' experiences instead of structured content, occasionally use train-ing techniques that are outside your comfort zone, and of course, do your own job before you accuse someone else of not doing theirs.

The story also has a few other elements of note. If you have ever conducted training before, you may empathize and feel anxious as the story evolves. Where are the books? Will she get them in time? How is she going to make up for the missed content? That anticipation triggered by an unknown outcome makes the listener want to hear more. When the end does come, it is amusing, primarily because it is unexpected and has a dash of self-deprecating humor—the person who was initially perceived as a victim surrounded by incompetence was actually helped by literally everyone and would have known that had she arrived to work early enough to stop by her desk.

Stories we find surprising or amusing are entertaining to us. But do stories have to be entertaining, and should we intentionally make them so? The characteristics we are exploring are tools you can use to help craft a story so that it is more likely to achieve a specific outcome. "Entertainment" is one of those tools, but it is a different story quality than the others I have described because its role is to enhance what is already there. This is an important distinction; in a learning context, humor should enhance the content, not be the content. For example, a relevant, but dry, story may still be helpful, but an amusing story that's irrelevant, while fun to listen to, may not improve performance. A meaningful story can be made more memorable and effective if the storyteller highlights what is amusing or surprising about the events that the story describes. This chapter explores strategies for enhancing stories with a dash of the unexpected.

Why Entertainment Matters in Stories

Your favorite comedian tells a story about how a surprise birthday party he planned for his girlfriend went horribly—and hilariously—wrong. A five-year-old describes her day in the most incoherent way imaginable as you nod, emote, and otherwise pretend to follow along. Public television airs a comprehensive documentary filled with intimate first-person accounts of the Vietnam War, a topic that's always fascinated you. You may derive the same enjoyment from each of these events—funny, awkward (but adorable!), or tragic—because they are all entertaining.

What does "entertaining" mean? We know it when we see it—or feel it—but with no consistent definition, it is difficult to develop strategies to be entertaining. Perhaps we can all agree that the feeling of being entertained is a pleasurable one—the comedy that makes us laugh may be just as pleasing as the melodrama that makes us cry.

However, we must also remember that relevant content and meaningful activities are the most important characteristics of a well-designed course. So, while entertainment may play a supporting role, knowing how and when to make a story entertaining is a useful teaching strategy in every facilitator's bag of tricks. Here, to narrow our focus, I'm specifically looking at entertaining stories that rely on surprise or amusement.

How Entertainment Contributes to Facilitating Learning

Some instructors are so entertaining that their witty observations are more memorable than the content. Yet others believe that humor and other gimmicks impede learning. No one is suggesting that you learn how to be a stand-up comic, but being strategically entertaining is useful for many reasons:

- It facilitates learning and memory.
- It creates and reinforces relationships.
- It relieves interpersonal tension that may distract from learning.

Entertainment Facilitates Memorization and Learning

Learning and memorizing are not synonymous, but memory is an essential part of the learning process. Entertaining stories trigger emotions, and participants are more likely to remember experiences that tap into their feelings. In her book, *Stories for Work: The Essential Guide to Business Storytelling,* Gabrielle Dolon (2017) writes, "Emotional arousal, not the importance of the information, helps memory."

It is not necessarily the experience you are describing in your story that triggers emotions; it's the experience you create when you shape and tell the story. There may be nothing unusual about your story's events. What matters is that you describe how the events changed you, and how well the listeners personally relate to that change.

In addition to remembering the story events, listeners also remember the content the story supports, which is the point of telling the story in the first place. If you are teaching a course on intercultural communication, learners will remember not only your story about what you learned while teaching overseas, but how what you learned in the story supports your larger point. This is another reason why it is important to be intentional about the stories you select and to consider how well they convey the point you are attempting to communicate. The link between your story and the content should be obvious.

Entertainment Creates and Reinforces Relationships

The facilitator-learner relationship often reflects the superior-subordinate paradigm that most of us learned in grade school. Adult learning facilitators use a variety of strategies to maintain some sort of control over the in-class experience while simultaneously trying to break free of the idea that instructors are authority figures who know all. A reason why this hierarchical relationship is ineffective is because, regardless of the topic, adult learners bring experience to the table and facilitators who respect that want learners to contribute their experiences freely. Participant contributions enhance the course and help learners connect with and understand new content. While the facilitator's experience may be more relevant, it is often no more valuable than anyone else's in the room.

Leveling the facilitator-learner relationship is a delicate process. While it may be easier for everyone if we all saw one another as peers, the participants are probably paying quite a bit of money and devoting a lot of time to hearing from an expert, not a peer. Consequently, it takes more than a couple of well-placed, "Hello, fellow learners! I'm one of you!" proclamations for participants to see a facilitator as one of them. The most effective strategy is to be yourself—another professional who simply had the opportunity to learn a skill at a greater depth or breadth, or, at the very least, to master the art of facilitation.

Telling a story has a way of disabusing preconceived notions of who people are and are not. Stories peel back the layers to reveal how a person learned what they know: practice, time, and honest reflection. But stories are not "humanizing" by default. The story should be intentionally selected and shaped to demonstrate the vulnerability, fear, and hope we all face when balancing risk with reward.

Stories shine when they are both revealing and entertaining. Self-deprecating humor works well in these cases. In fact, if you're telling a story that includes unsettling events, adding levity may be essential, and because people are only hearing your side of the story, the best target is you. However, remember that using humor is always tricky, and while self-deprecating humor may be the most innocuous—who would complain that you are making fun of yourself—it does have its downsides. Several studies have explored whether self-deprecating humor serves its purpose, which is typically to present modesty and be considered more likable, and while most have determined it works, it's only under certain circumstances. For example, one study conducted at the University of New Mexico concluded that the success of self-deprecating humor is influenced by the status of the person making the joke—the higher the status, the more effective the joke.

Entertaining stories not only humanize the instructor; the shared experience of laughter also binds participants. In his book, *Laughter: A Scientific Investigation,* Robert R. Provine (2001) writes that "laughter is primarily a social vocalization that binds people together. It is a hidden language that we all speak. It is not a learned group reaction but an instinctive behavior programmed by our genes. Laughter bonds us through humor and play." Creating an environment where everyone feels comfortable laughing and swapping stories with one another is fuel for learning.

Entertainment Relieves Tension

Putting adults in a classroom when they are still haunted by the ghosts of school days past is a situation wrought with potential conflict. Adult learning principles suggest that adults want their experiences to be heard, validated, and included in the overall learning experience. How easy that is to do depends on a variety of factors, such as how much the learners may already know about the topic, how they feel about having to be there, and perhaps how they feel about the instructor. Combine those factors with individual personalities, the strength of wills, and anxiety about the unknown, and you never know what may happen. Sometimes the content is uncomfortable to talk about, or there are issues occurring within the company at large that are weighing heavily on people's minds. Or, perhaps it is the participants. It only takes one antagonizer—or as they would put it, someone who likes to "broaden" the discourse by playing devil's advocate—to turn a supportive environment into a problematic one.

In cases where tension runs so high that it affects everyone's ability to learn, tackling the issue head-on is always the answer, and I advocate getting to that place sooner rather than later. But, in the meantime—during that murky period between perception and reality—humor is a great way to de-escalate a situation, as long as your intent is clear to you and the participants. Just be careful that the humor is pointing to the content or the situation, never at the participant.

Stories Enhanced by Entertainment

Facilitators often tell me that they are not good storytellers because nothing interesting ever happens to them. If that is their perception of their lives, then, yes, that is a big barrier to selecting and shaping stories. We have explored story structure and a few of the elements that can make a story effective, but even with all the boxes checked off, it's the events the story describes that make it effective. While the best storytellers can make even the most mundane task interesting, it will clearly take more effort, talent, and imagination to make a trip to the grocery store as compelling as a story about ascending Mount Everest.

You do not need to be a swashbuckler to have entertaining stories to tell, but believing that some of your own stories are entertaining is critical to your success as a storyteller. If you believe an event is interesting, you are more likely to reflect on it and draw conclusions about what you have experienced. Events supported by the conclusions you draw from meaningful reflection separate an effective story from a self-indulgent one.

Exploring more and taking on more risks can lead to an interesting life—however you define that—and an interesting life may lead to more stories to tell. Whether you decide to take the risky route, play it safe, or land somewhere in between, the best way to discover your own interesting stories is to think about what is entertaining about the life you lead now and all that you have experienced, rather than simply scouring your life for an entertaining story. What you find boring, others may find fascinating and instructive. When you shape and tell your stories, believing that they are worth hearing is what makes them shine.

The stories you are looking for contain elements that may evoke a pleasurable experience either through suspense or amusement. The goal is to select and shape stories that are suspenseful or amusing.

Shaping Suspenseful Stories

In Jane Cleland's 2016 book *Mastering Suspense, Structure, and Plot: How to Write Gripping Stories That Keep Readers on the Edge of Their Seats,* she writes: "Suspense is the heart and soul of storytelling. . . . To keep your readers engaged, you need to tell a gripping story that involves relatable characters." Consider the story of the missing workbooks I mentioned in the beginning of this chapter. When I was actually living the events in the story, I was genuinely surprised that the books were by my desk the entire time. I expected you to be surprised as well. If I'd left out the part about how my perspective on teaching with workbooks changed, it would have been your classic story with an unexpected ending. It also would have simply been a string of events. Now, suppose I wanted to add a dash of suspense; what could I do differently?

A surprise is typically an unexpected occurrence: a loud crash from the kitchen when you are home alone, or a yearly bonus that was larger than anticipated. Suspense is a state or feeling of excited or anxious uncertainty about what may happen. Storytellers often create suspense as they lead the listener to the surprise. One technique is to reveal clues. For example, I intentionally left a few details out of my story about the missing workbooks, including the several times throughout that morning when I could have gone to my desk. There were a few supplies at my desk that I needed, but to save time, I got them from the supply closet instead. A co-worker stopped by and mentioned that my phone was ringing, but I didn't go look because class was starting. If I had revealed those clues, you may have suspected that there was a relationship between the missing books and my desk.

Another technique for ramping up suspense is to reveal the surprise first. Alfred Hitchcock said, "There is no terror in the bang, only in the anticipation of it." In Hitchcock's 1943 film *Shadow of a Doubt,* a possible serial murderer is hiding from the law at his sister's house with her family. Hitchcock does not lead us to believe that Uncle Charlie is a great guy and then surprise us at the end. We know when we first see him—in his small room with money strewn about and his landlord telling him that two men were asking for him—that he is a suspicious character. Hitchcock knew that the audience would feel anxiety as they wondered when and how Uncle Charlie's family would catch on. Then consider Hitchcock's 1948 film *Rope,* where within the first five minutes, we hear a man scream and see two other men strangling that man to death. Hitchcock knew the real suspense would be in us wondering why those two men murdered someone, and if they would pay for their crime.

A more practical example may be to begin the story with information that will surprise listeners, depending on what is reasonable for the context. It could be a surprise about the storyteller or a twist in the story. This works better if your story really has a truly unexpected event instead of just a coincidence. However, these are difficult to come by in a business context, where history tends to repeat itself. Other times, the surprise may not even be evident to you until you tell the story and ask people for their feedback—an event that is par for the course for you may be a suspenseful adventure for someone else.

Shaping Stories That Are Amusing

When I think of the entertaining stories I have heard, the amusing ones come to mind first. Doug Stevenson (2008) writes in his book *Story Theater Method:* "It's true for professionals and it's true for you as well. If you want to hold an audience's attention, ya gotta be funny. You don't have to be drop dead hilarious. But you do have to be humorous enough to get a few laughs every now and then."

I try to make my entertaining stories funny, but I'm often guilty of the classic mistakes, like adding more details until I get the response I want or laughing to signal that this is the funny part. My advice is to start with the truth and instead of trying to make it funny, find the funny in the truth.

So, what is funny? Deconstructing joy seems like a joyless activity, and yet there are volumes of research that do just that. The most common research approach is to explore the more objective and observable, "What makes people laugh?" instead of the very subjective and elusive, "What's funny?" Journalist Alison Beard (2014) writes, "We laugh when we find that something we've momentarily believed to be the case isn't in fact true, and at others in the same predicament, and at stories about such situations, especially if they are linked to pleasures of other kinds, such as insight, schadenfreude, superiority, or sexual titillation." Indeed, in *The Psychology of Humor: Theoretical Perspectives and Empirical Issues,* psychologist Patricia Keith-Spiegel (1964) lists some theories of why people laugh, including out of instinct, at incongruity, out of ambivalence, for release, when we solve a puzzle, to regress, when we're surprised, and to feel superior. Let's take a closer look at the last two.

Experiencing something that is unexpected (being surprised) may cause embarrassment, and as a result we often laugh to soothe our anxiety. Describing a shock as being "tricked" may seem like a bit much, but even something as innocent as a knock-knock joke is a trick that relies on deception and misdirection. Another theory called the benign violation theory states that we laugh when a surprise—or a "violation" of how we believe the world should be—is perceived as benign or harmless.

When we laugh at the expense of others, it makes us feel superior. This basic human desire can only be felt if a person has accomplished something amazing or by criticizing the amazing accomplishments of others. For most of us, the second option is easier. In fact, according to Mark Shatz and Mel Helitzer (2016), "The professional humorist must always be aware that audience members are happiest when his subject matter and technique encourage them to feel superior." But we are not always interested in laughing at people. Superiority mixed with empathy, sympathy, and congeniality also prompt laughter.

I am not suggesting that you dissect your stories to look for these characteristics, nor am I suggesting that you build stories around them. But as you shape your stories, you can enhance these characteristics as you come across them to get the type of reaction you want from content that is already present.

As you examine your stories and attempt to identify the entertaining elements, look for the unexpected. It does not have to be a big twist—just something that the listener doesn't expect. Once you have identified that, consider the best way to convey both the shock and the point of it. You may decide to add elements of suspense by revealing clues along the way, or you may want to go for humor and emphasize the absurdity of the twist or the events surrounding it. Remember to focus on shaping what is already present in the story instead of adding additional elements for shock value.

Checklist for Selecting Stories That Entertain

As you consider which stories to use, ask yourself, does your story:

✓ Build humor and suspense based on events native to the story (as opposed to events added for comedic effect)?

✓ Have elements of the unexpected?

✓ Have points of tension that lead up to a surprise?

Wrap-Up: What's So Funny?

Everyone wants their stories to be entertaining. The content matters, but so does enhancing the amusement, surprise, and suspense in your stories. Many public speaking books encourage you to avoid humor. It can be a slippery slope, and if you are not careful the joke will be on you. Instead, it is better to understand how humor and surprise work and to be strategic about using them. Focus on the characteristics that make your stories enjoyable and how entertainment affects the learning experience.

Entertainment facilitates memorization and learning, creates and reinforces relationships among the participants and with the instructor, and relieves tension that can often negatively affect the learning environment. While shaping your stories, make them entertaining by enhancing elements of surprise, suspense, and amusement.

PART 3

Telling Stories That Teach

he storytelling process begins with a meaningful experience, one that stays with you long after it is over. That lingering can lead to reflection, where you consider what happened, what it means, and how you've changed as a result. An experience filtered through reflection creates a story that becomes a part of you, for better or worse, and it is uniquely yours. As time passes and more experiences evolve into stories, some will encroach on the space of the older ones and challenge your initial conclusions on your way to creating new ones. At some point, these living, breathing, ever-morphing stories that have informed your decisions will be ready to begin informing the decisions of others. This is the time to share your story.

Part 1 explored shaping stories, and part 2 featured a few characteristics that stories used to teach should have. Part 3 is devoted to telling those stories. There are many books on public speaking and storytelling, and the guidance they provide is useful. Other books talk about how to conduct instructor-led training in classrooms. This section explores the space between public speaking and teaching. Facilitators do not give speeches, and traditional teaching strategies are sometimes at odds with storytelling techniques. Facilitating with story is a delivery style unto itself.

8

Storytellers Who Reveal Themselves

I may have looked calm on the outside as I stared out at the 100 or so people who attended the session I was delivering on becoming a freelancer, but on the inside, I was having an existential crisis. Questions kept popping into my head. Why was I freelancing? What was I sacrificing to do this? Why couldn't I have just been happy I had a job, and accept that we all have to take the good with the bad? Why was I so hung up on being free? What was I trying to prove?

When I first agreed to deliver the presentation on starting a freelance career, I had no idea that it would spark these feelings of self-doubt. All I knew was that resigning from full-time employment to freelance was the best decision I'd ever made. I was my own boss and I set my own hours. There were a few drawbacks, but if you could find work and work could find you, what drawback was worth giving up your freedom to be an employee? I was living what so many people saw as the end goal, a distant dream they were now working toward. I could not wait to tell them stories about my experiences, which I had already selected and shaped for the presentation.

By this point in my career, I had been freelancing full time for three years. I had learned a few things in that time that I wish I had known before I started the journey. Well, in truth, I did know about them before I quit my job, but I chose to ignore them because they did not fit into the narrative I created for myself. I was jumping anyway, and I was not willing to wait. I remember saying to a friend, "What's the worst that could happen?"

I knew that many session participants might not listen to my cautionary tales, and I didn't want them to make the same mistakes I had, so I decided to create a handout that listed all the things a professional would be giving up by walking away from a full-time job. I should not have done that. While listing everything I had given up to be a freelancer, I began to ask myself the question I wanted the presentation participants to consider: Is it worth it?

It was such an honor to be selected to conduct this session, but on that day, all I could think about was how, although my conference admittance was free, I did not have an employer to pay for my hotel, flight, and expenses. And, I was not collecting a salary while I was there, like most of the attendees sitting in front of me. I began second-guessing my decision to begin freelancing.

If a story's events can tap into the emotions of the listener, one can only imagine what sharing those events will do to the storyteller who is reliving the experiences and the feelings they evoke. Regardless of what the story is about, its events and how the speaker feels about those events are two different things. Remember, no matter how inconsequential you believe the story is, you remember it and feel compelled to tell it for a reason.

For me, the conflict between the sudden and unexpected feelings of disappointment at freelancing and my desire to speak positively about making this choice created a cognitive dissonance that could not be resolved in front of an audience. What happens when you have an unresolved internal conflict, but have to pick a side anyway? You'll begin to question whether you believe what you are saying, and whether the listeners should believe what you're saying. Are you telling your truth? Are you being authentic?

What It Means to Be Authentic

We have all met people who come across as "real." They are the "what you see is what you get" people with no hidden agenda. They say what they mean and mean what they say, for better or worse. We believe these people are authentic, but what does "authentic" mean? If we all agreed on the dictionary definition—"to be genuine"—then why might a person who seems genuine to one person upon the first meeting seem like a fraud to someone else? At the risk of sounding like a self-help book, before we can explore how authenticity applies to storytelling, we must get on the same page about what it means.

We tend to assign authenticity as a characteristic, like tall or short. The danger is that just as tall people are always tall, we assume that authentic people will always demonstrate that attribute. Because authenticity is seen as a positive trait, we tend to view authentic people in a positive light. We also assume the inverse is true—those who do not possess the authenticity gene are viewed as less trustworthy. Worse, when we project these assumptions onto others, we're proven wrong more than we would like to admit.

Authenticity is not the birthright of a blessed few. Brené Brown (2010), in her book *The Gifts of Imperfection: Let Go of Who You Think You're Supposed to Be and Embrace Who You Are,* calls authenticity "a practice—a conscious choice of how you want to live." She says, "It's about the choice to show up and be real. The choice to be honest. The choice to let our true selves be seen." It is something almost all of us work toward, day by day and choice by choice.

Philosophers, psychologists, and artists have pondered how to live authentically for centuries. Writings focus on having the courage to be who you truly are. For many people, being themselves is not a choice they consciously make, because there is no other way to be. It comes naturally. However, many others struggle with living life on their own terms every day—think about the countless songs, books, films, and other works of art dedicated to the desire and the cost of being oneself.

The battle for your authentic self is fought on all fronts, both the personal and the professional. For example, while I was sure about the content in my conference presentation on freelancing, my ambivalence about something deeply personal still affected what should have been an academic exercise. This chapter focuses on what it looks like to choose authenticity while you are telling your story in front of a group.

Authenticity and Facilitating

A high school English teacher I know once said, "When you close that classroom door, it's your show." She made the comment during a discussion about the teaching techniques we learned in graduate school. She thought those techniques rarely helped her in practical application when it was just her alone in a room with 30 teenagers. She had to make snap judgments that were guided more by her personal opinions and teaching philosophies than by any theories she learned in school. For her, having clarity about what she believed about behavioral issues was what she needed most—for example, students talking in class, philosophical perspectives on how Shakespeare depicted women, or academic dilemmas about whether an answer to an essay question was close enough.

The behavior that the content supports, reinforces, or diminishes is the reason why a class exists. But content does not teach. If content taught, we could simply project an automated PowerPoint presentation on a screen in front of a room full of participants and leave. Learning happens when participants are engaged, and facilitated experiences is one way to do that. So, the content alone is not enough. If I am leading a class through content, I need to show up somewhere. My experiences will permeate the message even when I am not telling a story. How I feel or what I believe about the content will influence how I teach, how I answer questions, and then, ultimately, how participants learn. With so much at stake, it is important to gain insight into your truth.

Authenticity in facilitation is about knowing what you believe and how you feel about the experiences you have had that are related to the content you are teaching. Participants who are watching and listening can detect the feelings you believe you are hiding or do not know are there. People are typically generous and will not penalize you for being passionate about a topic—they may empathize with your telltale signs of boredom, or share your frustration as you discuss those preventable corporate problems that never seem to go away—but they will not forgive a con job. They do not want you to tell them something is real when you clearly do not believe it yourself. They will dismiss, along with your credibility, any stories that do not ring true. They want authenticity.

Resolve Your Feelings

In her book, *Long Story Short: The Only Storytelling Guide You'll Ever Need,* Margot Leitman (2015) recommends, "If you're not 'over it,' don't tell it." If "over it" means no longer being affected by the events that transpired in the selected story, I would not have many stories to share! To her point, however, if you are still angry, sad, or even extraordinarily happy or excited about the events in your story, then it may pour out of your mouth as a muddled mess, despite all your planning and practicing.

My session on freelancing is a good example of what could happen when you unintentionally tap into unresolved emotions. Starting your own business and then running it full time is a life-changing decision, one that affects every aspect of your existence. I did not realize the enormity of that fact when I first went out on my own and, in retrospect, I was not ready for what was to come. And although I recognized those feelings before agreeing to do the presentation, a part of me knew that I was not actually ready to talk about it. Sure, I could have casual conversations about freelancing. I was happy to offer advice to the many people who asked how I got started. But I was not ready to spend an hour promoting freelancing to a large group of people.

I do not believe that being "over" the emotions triggered by a story is a requirement for telling the story. But you should have some distance (physical, mental, and chronological) from the events, and take the time to reflect on what happened so you can come to some sort of conclusion regarding your feelings. Ideally, you should go a step beyond a conclusion and land on a resolution. That resolution—being at peace with why the event or change happened and how you have changed as a result—is the story's purpose. That information will ultimately answer the question, "Why are you telling this story?" for the listener. Of course, this should happen before you add the story to your playlist.

Getting Closer to "Over It"

All you can do is tell the truth as you know it right now. While the "truth" is present because the story is factual, only you know the veracity of your version of the story and how the events affected you. Only you know whether you are being authentic—the listeners will only know what you say and how you say it. They will judge this experience by their own criteria based on what they know to be true.

Body language that contradicts what you are saying is a sure sign that something is amiss. If you say you are happy but your posture and movements tell a different story, your internal battle may come out in what you say or how you say it. Perhaps you make sarcastic remarks or you overexplain as if you are trying to convince both the listener and yourself. There is no guarantee that being your true self as you facilitate will help participants learn, but seeing or sensing that you are working through your own issue as you facilitate is distracting at best and diminishes your credibility at worst—both of which affect the learning experience your stories are intended to enhance.

The point is not for you to resolve open issues before sharing stories about them. The goal is to know where you stand. Again, while it's ideal for this to happen earlier in the process, it's often not until you are preparing to tell the story that alarm bells go off. Let's look at a few strategies to determine whether you've resolved a story before you tell it:

- **Respect your feelings:** When it comes to business, nothing is personal, right? Business and feelings play no role in strategic decisions, right? Perhaps. Perhaps not. It doesn't matter. You have the right to feel how you feel. If you feel disappointed, those feelings should not be diminished just because what happened was for the good of the company. Suppressed or ignored feelings tend to manifest in other ways. If you have unresolved feelings about a story or topic, they may show up during your session. Allow yourself to feel without apology. The good news is that while you have little control over how you feel, you can control how you respond to those feelings.

- **Be honest:** Be realistic about how long it may take to recover from any upheaval in your life. No matter who you are, if the wound is fresh, it probably still stings. I once got laid off from a job that I had planned to quit. It never occurred to me that I would be angry until I started talking about it to people. I should be happy. I wanted to leave, and I not only got my wish, I got severance too. But how dare they quit me first! Regardless of what I knew about what I felt, it would have been unwise of me to build a story off the event so soon after it happened.

- **Find your threshold:** If you think you are ready to tell your story, determine whether there are limitations to where you can use it. Say your story to yourself. If you can get through that without going off the rails, say it in a mirror. Tell it to one friend. And finally, tell it to a group of people that consists of friends and strangers. Perhaps you'll find that you can tell the story, but only in certain circumstances. I have tried this technique many times. I will tell friends what I believe is a delightful, funny story, only to have them ask me, much to my surprise, what I am so angry about!

Trust the People in the Room. Trust Yourself.

To trust is to believe that someone or something is consistently able, truthful, and reliable. Trust is valuable. It should be protected, and, once it is lost, it is difficult to recover. We all have differing approaches to giving and earning trust—some believe that it is difficult to give full trust until it is earned, while others assume good intentions from the beginning and give trust freely. Then there are those in the middle who recognize the risk of trusting liberally, but still give the benefit of the doubt.

We want to trust and work hard to get to a place where the process becomes easier for us. It feels good to believe in something real. In fact, trusting a person says just as much about the trustee as it does the person doing the trusting. Consider the times when your trust was violated and you blamed yourself more than the person who let you down. We want to believe we can make the right choices and are smart enough not to be tricked. We want to trust ourselves.

We know the benefits of using trust wisely, but the benefit relevant to facilitation is that the ability to trust makes room for, perhaps even fuels, vulnerability. To be vulnerable is to be exposed to the possibility of being attacked or harmed. If it sounds scary, that's because it is. I want to be clear that I know that there are people for whom vulnerability—physical, economical, or social, for example—is not a choice. I am distinguishing between a *vulnerability* that truly puts you at risk and a *purposeful vulnerability* that manifests positively. But the official definition of vulnerability still works for a facilitator's journey. You're still "exposed," but the "possibility of being attacked or harmed" is relative.

Allow for Your Own Vulnerability

No matter how much I believe facilitating learning does not require instructors to be experts, I still do not want to be wrong about something I should know. And every time I get in front of a group to speak, I run the risk of making errors.

The personal nature of storytelling only increases those feelings of vulnerability. A concern when telling a story about ourselves is how we will be perceived based on the information we share. If your story is about how an action you took "saved the day," will people see you as arrogant? If you downplay your role, will people think you are fishing for compliments? If the story is about you embarrassing yourself, will people see you as irresponsible or relatable? Sometimes I am so taken aback by how people interpret my stories, I wonder if we are hearing the same words. When someone doubts or otherwise criticizes your facts, they can look them up. When someone criticizes your story, it feels as if it is a criticism of you.

Vulnerability does not just relate to emotion in the traditional sense. It could also be giving yourself permission to be wrong. Perhaps it is admitting to the class that you do not know the answer. Maybe it is conceding that facilitators must walk the tightrope of letting go of power while maintaining control of the classroom. It's being comfortable with discomfort.

Build a Relationship

We often worry that we are going to say the "wrong" thing. You may be more concerned about saying the wrong thing to another person than you are about saying too much about yourself. Perhaps that is true. But while we are concerned about hurting someone's feelings, we are probably more worried about being seen as the type of person who would say such things about someone out loud. This fear goes back to accidentally revealing our true selves—or at least revealing traits that someone believes are our true selves.

When you facilitate or teach in any capacity, you enter into a relationship with the participants. That relationship is forged by having a shared goal, and its success depends on open communication. Like all relationships, you want to know who you are getting into a relationship with—you want to know who your students are, and vice versa. I often think about what this business of training and being trained requires of us. Learners are supposed to believe what a stranger says, simply because they are standing in the front of the room. They are also expected to share their stories with the other strangers in the room.

I am supposed to believe that we are all acting in good faith while sharing my stories, knowledge, and energy with—again—a group of people I have never seen before and may never see again. My career has essentially been built on teaching strangers, regardless of whether I was working inside a company as an employee, working outside a company as a freelancer, or teaching a public course. While the exercise of going around the room and asking people to share who they are feels like it goes on way too long, I rarely facilitate in situations where the participants know one another or the facilitator. And yet, we must trust one another immediately if our relationship is going to yield the outcome we seek.

You will say the wrong things and so will they. You will embarrass yourself and so will they. The people in the room facing you are taking a far bigger risk than you are. They are handing over to you something precious—their time, attention, and energy. The least you can do is give them the truth, your truth, and a path to their own. How? Here is a three-step process: Take a deep breath. Trust yourself. Let go.

Checklist for Becoming an Authentic Storyteller

As you prepare to deliver your stories, ask yourself, are you:

- ✓ Prepared to facilitate with authenticity as your primary goal?
- ✓ Ready to allow yourself to be vulnerable and create an environment where your participants can be vulnerable too?
- ✓ Able to trust yourself and your participants?
- ✓ Able to value the relationship you are entering into?

Wrap-Up: The Value of Authenticity

As you facilitate with story, it is important to explore the value of being authentic and purposely vulnerable. Part of feeling safe while being vulnerable is to resolve your feelings about stories before you tell them. The process also involves a great deal of trust and relationship building with your participants. If you choose purposeful vulnerability, the key is to allow yourself the freedom to create a safe environment for your participants to follow your lead.

9

Storytellers Who Invite Listeners In

e heard the classroom door close behind us, and we all looked back. Samantha, our instructor, stood in the back of the room and said, "I once lost a quarter of a million dollars. I had $250,000 on a Monday, and it was gone on a Tuesday."

On her way to the front of the room, she stopped by each table, selected one person, and knelt down. Looking the first person in the eye, Samantha asked, "What would you do with $250,000?" Put on the spot, he said he didn't know. After that, people were ready with answers, which ranged from "Save it" to "Blow it all on a monthlong vacation." Soon, several people from each table Samantha was visiting offered answers, and she would respond to everyone with follow-up questions, quips, or sometimes just a smile. By the time she arrived at the front of the room, we had all considered what we would do with the money. It did not matter that it was money that we did not have (or had lost)—we all shared in her disappointment before she even told us how she lost the money. We were invested.

I had signed up to be a participant in this sales class after freelancing for a few years, but I had not been looking forward to it. Bored with reading books and watching sales pitch videos online, I wanted to learn in a classroom, at a table with like-minded people and an instructor at the front of the room. It's not that I'm a people person, but I am a story person, and every time I'm in a full classroom, I'm surrounded by them.

As I headed for an empty seat, a bright smile attached to a woman dressed in a blue and white polka-dot dress appeared out of nowhere, intercepting me. "Hello, I'm Samantha. Just find a seat anywhere," she said, and walked away. A little disoriented, I heard, "How about right here?" coming from my right at a distance that Samantha must have traveled at warp speed. I walked over to her and sat at a nearby table with three other people wearing uneasy smiles who were no doubt also commandeered by Samantha.

Soon, nearly all the tables were full, and I noticed that Samantha was missing. It was then that she emerged from the back of the room and announced that she'd lost a quarter of a million dollars. It was only after she methodically moved to the front, engaging with the group along the way, that she finally told us her story about a professional services sale gone wrong. Years before, she got a lead on an opportunity that was tailor-made for her. Everything was in place—she understood the client's business, she had a long-standing relationship with her contact, and they were ready to buy. However, she did not rattle off that list of advantages when she told her story. Instead, she said, "The situation couldn't have been more perfect. You tell me. What's your ideal sales scenario?" We listed ideal situations, and she would respond by agreeing or further discussing the participant's point. After telling us a little more of the story, she asked us to list what we thought had gone wrong. We learned that she misread cues, followed up too late, and either said too much or too little. These were also among the suggestions she solicited from us.

Even after the initial telling of the story, she kept going back to it as she taught us sales concepts throughout the morning. Her story and how she told it created a shared context for the class, and whoever referred to it was immediately understood. Her story became our story—which later became the story we all had of that day. Afterward, I asked her how she came up with the technique.

"What technique?" she asked.

I said, "You know. The one where you include participants in your stories."

She said that she tells most of her stories that way. After teaching for a few years, she became bored with her own stories, so she started asking people to guess the outcomes to mix things up.

"Then I saw that people might not have remembered the stuff I taught them, but they remembered that story," she said. "People were acting like my story happened to them."

What It Means to Let Others In

We have explored the idea that once you tell a story, it no longer belongs to you. Somewhere between you telling the story and the listener hearing it, your story transforms and the listeners are not hearing the story that you know so well—they are constructing their own versions of the experience you are shaping. No matter how structured and precise you are, the listeners will filter your words through their own experiences. At best, they will remember key events—at worst, they will immediately make a judgment and hear something entirely different.

Have you ever been so attached to a story that it infuriated you if anyone said anything to you while you were telling it? I know I have said, "Please just let me finish the story" countless times, especially when I want to tell the story a certain way. We have this idea that people should listen quietly to our stories from beginning to end. Perhaps we learned this as children, when our parents or teachers read us stories and made it clear that our job was to listen and suppress those questions about what Rumpelstiltskin's deal was anyway. Yet, one of the best parts of watching a television show or movie is talking about what is happening on the screen as it is happening. We ask the characters questions like, "What are you doing?" or make declarative statements like, "He's right behind you!" or "Don't open that door!" We long for inclusion, even if we have to imagine it.

It is frustrating to know that you are not being heard as you intended, but it does not matter once you accept that stories are not real. The events and people are real (usually), but as we've already discussed, the story itself lives in a space between what is true and what you believe is true. We have all witnessed an event with a friend and then later compared notes only to find that while you agree on the basics—you were both on the train and there was a man in a clown suit on the train with you—you disagree on your impression of how menacing he looked or even the color of his hair. The story you tell is shaped more by the impression than the facts. Embracing that your version, or impression, of the story is the *true* (with a small "t") version and the only one you can ever tell can work to your advantage when you facilitate with story.

Facilitating to Include Others in Your Stories

On the second day of my sales training course, I came back early from lunch. Samantha was there early, too, answering emails. We chatted a bit, and I learned a few things about her. She was a salesperson who decided to supplement her income by doing training on the side. She did not know that there was such a thing as a trained facilitator when I asked if she was one, and she thought she was a good facilitator because she liked people. She also said that she did not like to overthink her process. I told her not to worry; I would do it for her.

All trainers should take classes on selling. In his book *To Sell Is Human: The Surprising Truth About Moving Others,* Daniel Pink (2012) writes, "People are now spending about 40 percent of their time at work engaged in non-sales selling—persuading, influencing, and convincing others in ways that don't involve anyone making a purchase." In my role as either a facilitator or an instructional designer, "persuading, influencing, and convincing others" could be added to my job description. While I would prefer for my expertise to be accepted immediately, that rarely happens, and I am not so sure it should.

To teach someone a skill, I must sell that person on the value of that skill and then convince them that the way I am recommending they carry it out is the best way. And I have to show them that I am a person to trust. Storytelling can serve these purposes:

- Facilitators can use stories that **demonstrate the value of a skill** in context. For example, the story could show how essential it is for managers to communicate frequently with their staff.
- Facilitators can use stories to **explain the advantages and disadvantages of different alternatives,** and consequently reinforce why their recommendation may lead to the better outcome. The story could demonstrate the difference between communicating like a leader who inspires and a manager who gives orders.
- Facilitators could use a personal story about leadership communication **strategies** and their experiences using them.

You may start by focusing these stories on you and your experiences if you don't have enough information about the participants. But your goal is to discuss your experiences in a way that demonstrates how your knowledge and experience relate to what is true for the participants. The ideal approach is to tap into their perspectives so that you can incorporate their experiences into your story. Sales professionals already know this. They work to sell experiences instead of objects, just as you should focus less on selling content and focus more on selling the experience of using the content. A car salesperson is not selling you a car. She is selling you the new life you will have with that car. This is also true for selling services. As a consultant, I am not selling you tasks. I am selling you on the promise those tasks fulfill, which will ultimately result in the solution you need.

Inviting learners into your stories is another way to engage them, which is essential to the learning experience. While selecting and shaping your stories, start considering when, where, and how listeners can enter and what cues you will give them. The more relatable your story is initially, the easier it will be to find areas where your participants can contribute. In fact, going through this exercise as you shape your story can also help you ensure that it is relatable before you tell it.

Another benefit to letting people into your stories is that their contributions can enhance elements of stories that you have been telling for years. I have a story about working with a difficult subject matter expert. He was antagonizing and obnoxious, but by the end of the project, we became friends. The message of the story when I first shaped it was how time changes relationships. However, every time I told the story and invited others in, I was forced to dig deeper—I never considered why our relationship changed. Since then, by soliciting listener contributions, this story has evolved into several stories about fear, power, and trust.

Asking for Contributions

Once you accept the challenge of letting others share in your stories, you must develop a process for doing it. The process should include both when to solicit them and how to ask. But, don't force this process. It should feel authentic.

When to Ask

Search your story for meaningful contribution points that encourage the listeners to reflect on their experiences, contribute relevant information, and make a judgment among reasonable alternatives.

Ensure that your story remains intact, even with the contribution of other insights. You'll need to avoid asking for contributions around key plot points.

How to Ask for Contributions

How you ask for the contribution depends on what type of contribution you are looking for. If you want people to reflect on their experiences, try asking something like, "Could someone give me an example of when this happened to you?" Asking, "What are a few options for handling a situation like this?" will help you enhance the content. Participant contributions can also help you discuss alternative situations: "What would be the consequences of choosing option A over option B?"

Let Go of Your Stories

Chapter 8 ended with a plea to let go—let go of the fear of revealing who you are through telling your stories. Now, in addition to letting go, I am asking you to give something away. I am asking you to take an experience that happened to you and give it to someone else.

Consider Samantha again. I have experienced sales training as a facilitator, instructional designer, observer, and participant. Sales is a competitive field, one that tends to attract people who like to win. Consequently, they typically do not like to admit their shortcomings in public. In all my years interviewing sales subject matter experts for input on sales training programs I've designed, I've heard two types of stories from participants. The story either features the salesperson going up against impossible odds and emerging victorious, or is about the errors some other salesperson made. I rarely heard stories about their failures or the sales that they lost. And because they are rewarded by quickly moving on to the next opportunity after losing a sale, the ones who did talk about failure did not have much reflection to share. Onward and upward!

Within the narrative of the stories you tell about your experiences and how you responded to them is a commentary on your identity. By holding on to who you want the world to believe you are, you try to control that narrative. It is difficult to let go of something you believe belongs to only you. Letting the narrative go is a necessary first step before you can invite people in to contribute. Samantha did not care that her first story was about a failure, because she had long let go of the idea that one failure made her one. She included heroic tales in the session as well, but only to demonstrate what she had learned from her mistakes.

Ask

I get it. You have six hours of content and three hours to teach it. The only "known" in this scenario is the content, and that content needs to be told to participants. Asking and addressing open-ended questions may affect your schedule. Perhaps the content is so new or routine that you do not anticipate learners asking questions. In my experience, facilitators asking questions—extemporaneous questions, not preplanned questions written in the leader's guide—is becoming a lost art.

If you are not comfortable asking content-related questions, then asking questions while you are telling a story will be a challenge. You may not even realize you are not asking questions because you are so focused on the content. The next time you facilitate, count how many times you ask questions that are not polling, closed-ended questions, or questions you intend to answer yourself. Follow-up questions and other interactions instigated by learners also don't count. No matter what number you land on, don't settle. Ask more questions! The closer you can get to making your course feel like a conversation, the better.

The simplest way to start is to ask "what if" questions or questions about how the content relates to the participants' experience. Yes, someone may say something that derails your class—questions are variables that present risks. But if you believe that hearing you talk for three straight hours is helping participants improve performance, think again. Not only is performance probably not being positively influenced, but it is not up to you to connect the content to their experience. You cannot do it without knowing what their experience is. You can share your ideas on those connections, but your job is to facilitate the process of participants coming to their own conclusions.

Be Quiet

Once you ask a question, wait for the answer. Only speak if you sense that the question needs clarification. I know it sounds so simple, right? Some facilitators ask questions, give up too soon, and then answer the questions themselves because the silence is too uncomfortable. Get comfortable with silence and trust the process. This will be difficult, especially early in your career, but it gets easier with experience. It also makes participants uncomfortable; eventually, once they see you are not going to budge, someone will take one for the team and either answer the question or ask a follow-up question. You must get out of the way.

Checklist for Inviting Listeners In

As you prepare to deliver your stories, ask yourself, are you:
✓ Letting go of your stories?
✓ Asking participants to help you create a new shared experience?
✓ Being patient and quiet as participants answer your questions with their own contributions?

Wrap-Up: Make Something New Together

To create a new experience together, try developing ways to let your learners into your stories. Storytelling doesn't have to be a one-way experience. Adopting this philosophy diminishes the desire to just talk at your participants. The challenge is the concern that if you give up control of your stories, you give up control of the narrative you are using to communicate who you are. Let that idea go. Once the story leaves your mouth, it is no longer yours.

Before you invite participants into your stories, you need a process for doing so. Consider how and when you are going to ask people to join you. You will be in charge of helping participants navigate through this process, something that takes forethought and consideration for the position you are putting them in. Finally, once you ask participants to share, be quiet and let them contribute at their own pace. Remember, they need time to connect their experiences to your stories and the content.

10

Storytellers Who Use Body Language as a Tool

erhaps Kim and Lee did not know how drastically their styles differed before they team-taught a course in persuasion. Lee was my co-worker and had been a trainer for his entire career. Kim worked in marketing and dabbled in training. Lee intended to interview her as a subject matter expert and then work with me, an instructional designer, to build a class based on Kim's experiences using persuasion techniques in marketing. But Kim took over the project and decided that she wanted to facilitate, too. Instead of discouraging her, Lee asked our manager if I could observe the class to see whether together they had made a masterpiece or a mess. I am sure Lee's ideal outcome was that I would get Kim booted out of the classroom. I did not know what to expect, but could not wait to see it.

The morning of the class, Kim greeted everyone as they walked through the door, while Lee paced near the podium, stopping only to stare at people taking their seats as if he were deeply invested in where they landed. At 9 o'clock, Lee opened the course with the standard housekeeping rundown: "Donuts are here," "Bathroom is there," "I am this," "You are that," and "This is what we are going to do today." He had gone through the drill a thousand times and it showed, both in his high level of experience and his low level of enthusiasm.

When Lee introduced Kim, her wide smile and frantic wave lit up the space around her. As Lee soldiered on, unpersuasively, through the opening content on persuasion, Kim sat nearby, nodding, pacing, and laughing on cue, handily stealing focus. I stared at her the entire time, perhaps looking for reassurance that all of us—both Lee and the class—were going to get through this.

"OK, you've heard enough from me. I'll pass it over to Kim for this next part," Lee announced.

Kim took over, bursting through our boredom, beaming. The energy change caused the people at my table to shift in their seats. They sat up straight and leaned forward. There was a sense that she very badly wanted to be liked and it was a metaexperience to learn about persuasion while being persuaded. Unfortunately, after the novelty wore off it became apparent that Kim was not the savior we were waiting for. She was everything she should be—engaging, funny, and personable—but she seemed to be more interested in being in the spotlight than facilitating.

The morning flew by—shifting from introverted calmness to extroverted explosions exhausted all of us. There was no strategic method to this madness, but the universe has a way of forcing chaos into order. Kim, with her energy and her ability to command a room, organically emerged when order was needed. She effortlessly delivered content and managed activities. Otherwise, she only occasionally broke the fourth wall to acknowledge us. She rarely initiated interactions with the group and seemed to look through us instead of at us. Yet, her confident tone and manic gesticulating kept my attention through her long monologues.

Lee, however, became our advocate, working to ensure that we did not drown in Kim's content tsunami. His portion of the content mostly comprised questions about how the content related to our work lives. He seemed interested in how we were managing all the information Kim was sharing, and seemed to have an innate ability to sense confusion in the air. He would often ask questions that were so spot on they were immediately followed with sighs, furious nodding, or hushed murmurs of, "That's what

I was thinking." Throughout, his calm voice and minimalist approach to movement kept the ship steady.

Ultimately, it was a split decision. This course needed both of their approaches to facilitating. We would not have survived Lee's subdued style any more than we would have learned from Kim's. Still, I would have preferred both styles in one person.

Since then, I have seen many courses team-taught by two people, but I have never seen two people who were so different teach together. That's probably why I remember it so well. I came away from the experience thinking about how two people could approach the same content so differently. But their styles reflected their approaches to being in this world and filling the space they occupied.

Body Language and Facilitating With Story

We have explored letting go, showing up, and revealing who you are while you facilitate with story. But, when it comes to the most powerful visual tool you have—the tool that can add, enhance, or diminish what you say— more awareness is required. That tool is your body.

In his book *What Every BODY Is Saying: An Ex-FBI Agent's Guide to Speed-Reading People,* Joe Navarro (2008) writes:

> Nonverbal communication can also reveal a person's true thoughts, feelings, and intentions. For this reason, nonverbal behaviors are sometimes referred to as tells (they tell us about the person's true state of mind). Because people are not always aware they are communicating nonverbally, body language is often more honest than an individual's verbal pronouncements, which are consciously crafted to accomplish the speaker's objectives.

Many of the same guidelines that public speakers follow can be applied to storytelling and facilitating. In both cases, you are attempting to communicate clearly, engage the listeners, and bring your content to life. However, there are a few differences that should affect the intent behind the way you use your body:

- Ensure that your body language supports the message. Most presentations to large groups focus on one-way communication. Facilitators, however, want to encourage participation. Being behind a podium and asking, "Any questions?" will not get learners excited about pitching in.
- Understand how and when your body moves. Facilitation is also a more fluid and organic approach to delivering content, and requires more flexibility than a prepared speech. Because facilitating and storytelling can often be more animated than a standard presentation, you will need to have a greater awareness of how your body language can support your stories. Trainers need mental and, often, physical agility.

Instead of focusing on separate body parts or specific gestures, I will focus on intent. In other words, we will first consider the impression, mood, or commentary you want to communicate and then consider how you can use body language to create or reinforce it. There are two intents central to storytelling: creating intimacy and managing emotions.

Creating Intimacy

Many of us have witnessed a public event with a charismatic singer or a dynamic speaker, and thought, "It was like she was talking directly to me" or "I felt like I was the only person in the room." Perhaps it is the universal message behind their art that resonates with us. After all, so much of what we endure as individuals is similar to what we all go through—it just manifests in different ways.

The Dale Carnegie Training book, *Stand and Deliver: How to Become a Masterful Communicator and Public Speaker (2011),* advises that "The modern audience—whether it is fifteen people in a conference room or a thousand people in an arena or millions watching their televisions—wants speakers to talk directly and personally." Participants want to feel the same intimacy as a private interaction, regardless of the hundreds of people on either side of them. But they still want you, the presenter, to have the presence required to be in front of a group, and deliver with strength and confidence.

Storytelling can be a deeply personal act carried out in a very public space, and it is often easier to engage in it when there are mutual feelings of trust between the storyteller and the listener. One form of trust is intimacy. Unfortunately, how to establish intimacy with a group of people is another age-old, impossible-to-answer question. Everyone has different levers to pull and boundaries to cross. The most reliable tactic is to learn what most people have in common and, in that context, consider what resonates more with you. You cannot make people feel any more than you can make them learn. All you can do is consider what is true for you and use that knowledge to support an environment where intimacy is valued and fostered. There are two tools that can support intimacy: eye contact and physical proximity.

Eye Contact

I am passionate about eye contact because I spend so much time ensuring I make it, determining whether others are making it, and identifying how it can be used as a tool. When I'm facilitating, the participants' eyes tell me a lot about how the class is progressing. Am I going too fast or too slow? Am I confusing them or patronizing them? Am I lingering too long in some areas of the content? In interpersonal conversations, I am just as curious. Is this person enjoying our time together? Is the story going on too long? If I am telling a story and the listener's eyes are darting back and forth, I will assign meaning to that, whether or not there is any.

Public speaking courses teach that maintaining a moderate amount of eye contact is mandatory because it shows people that you are paying attention and are genuinely engaged. As a result, I have always believed that making eye contact should be a focus when learning how to facilitate. This is especially true if you're using stories, because of the connections you are attempting to make. However, the idea that more eye contact is always good is not accurate.

There is a perception that people who are lying have "shifty eyes" or otherwise tend to avoid making eye contact. If you believe that, then you are also more likely to believe that people who maintain consistent eye contact are telling the truth. But Navarro warns, "Keep in mind that predators and habitual liars actually engage in greater eye contact than most individuals, and will lock eyes with you."

There are also cultural reasons people avoid either giving or receiving direct and prolonged eye contact. In their study, "Eye Contact Perception in the West and East: A Cross-Cultural Study," Shota Uono and Jari K. Hietanen (2015) found that maintaining eye contact is not positively evaluated by people with East Asian cultural backgrounds. "In fact, in Japanese culture, people are taught not to maintain eye contact with others because too much eye contact is often considered disrespectful."

Despite these cautionary tales, I still believe that eye contact can be used as a tool to establish connections and reinforce intimacy. But, we must lean on the principle that we explored before—intent. Use eye contact to make connections, but be intentional about the impact you want to have on the listener. Don't indiscriminately use eye contact simply because you were told to in a speech class long ago. "Usually, the most effective way to use eye behaviors is to forget about them," advises Doug Lipman (1999), in his book *Improving Your Storytelling: Beyond the Basics for All Who Tell Stories in Work and Play.* "Instead, focus on your relationship to your audience and what you want to share or communicate with them. Then give yourself permission to use whatever eye behaviors seem to carry your storytelling forward."

Proximity

Returning to my opening story, as animated and energetic as Kim was, I think she must have been surrounded by an invisible force field, because she never stepped away from the podium while she lectured. In the small space she carved out for herself, she paced, acted out stories, and addressed people by name, but real interpersonal interaction with the group was where she drew the line. Lee, on the other hand, adeptly navigated the tables and chairs to reach people who asked questions so that he could talk to them face-to-face. He also came into the group when he acted out stories, spontaneously recruiting participants as co-stars.

Lee seemed to seek a personal relationship with each person who engaged with him. It was thrilling to watch him go from person to person, but I did worry that everyone else felt left out during these public one-on-ones. They were brief conversations, but while the person talking to Lee seemed connected, I felt like I was eavesdropping. My feedback to him at the time was to make sure the rest of us could see him. Now, my feedback would be for him to be more intentional about what he was trying to accomplish—was it to make one person feel connected or was it to create an environment where people felt supported enough to ask for what they needed? I am sure his answer would be "yes"—he wanted to do both. And he could do both by monitoring and modifying his distances and considering the experience he created for everyone by using his body and his position as a strategic tool.

What about the podium? I am obviously not going to tell you to remain in the podium's orbit, but I do know that some classroom setups require this. Nevertheless, remember, I am asking you to show up, facilitate, and tell stories from an authentic place. This requires mental and emotional exposure as well as physical. I have seen many great speakers tell amazing stories from a lectern. Videos of commencement speeches from actors, politicians, and leading businesspeople show how to touch the hearts and minds of a stadium full of people. We may even get choked up watching the video several years later—you cannot get more removed than that. But, let's consider this for a moment. The people who can change the world while standing still are typically people with a consistent message about themselves, what they do for a living, and how they demonstrate their value. What you see at that podium is not just a speech—it is who they are. They are clear about their intent and what they can offer the crowd. Be honest with yourself about your ability to move people. But for now, step away from the podium. Stop hiding.

Managing Emotions

If you have chosen to facilitate with a story that stirs your emotions, how you handle delivering these emotional parts is, again, a question about intent and what utility the story has. How do you want learners to feel? How do *you* want to feel?

You have two primary tools for conveying emotion using body language: your expressions and gesturing.

Expressions

Are you aware of how your face changes while you tell stories that conjure up emotions? Unless your job requires that level of awareness, you may have no idea. The current selfie culture has led to people becoming more aware of their angles than ever. But, those pictures are usually planned, and you probably take several shots before getting the right one. When you're talking in front of groups, you have less control over your expressions. You must become aware of how your face moves so that you can determine how it influences the way your message is perceived.

Authenticity applies to both story content and how the story is told. It is important that you take an organic approach to how you display emotions. The feeling comes first—the expression of that feeling comes second. In other words, you should allow your expressions to be triggered by reliving the experience you are describing in your story. However, describing how you were feeling is obviously different from experiencing it the first time. There is no need to jump for joy or break down sobbing (and if you feel the need to sob, this story is not ready to be told). Your goal is to communicate how you were feeling, not necessarily feel it—it could be unhealthy to hold on to some feelings, and even worse to have to publicly revisit them again and again. Chapter 8 explored how to resolve your feelings about a story if you believe you are in danger of losing control. The only way you will know what your expressions look like when you tell a story is to practice, ideally in front of a mirror.

Gestures

I am often struck by how a simple gesture can say so much. Like with facial expressions, the average person may pay little attention to how much they are gesturing during a conversation or presentation. People often say they "talk with their hands." However, if you are a facilitator and talk with your hands, you know how distracting it can be for the participants. You need to gain greater control over how your body reflects emotions so you can replicate those emotions when needed. Being aware of hand movement is not enough. You must understand how you occupy space.

There are four types of gestures. Knowing how each one can be used to your advantage can help enhance your stories:

- Iconic gestures show the concrete object or action that is being described, like using a throwing motion while describing throwing a ball. These gestures are used when acting out, not simply telling, your story. Instead of saying that you walked through a door, find the imaginary door in front of you, turn the handle, and walk through it.
- Metaphoric gestures show abstract concepts. An example may be holding out one palm to represent one point and then the other palm to represent a different point. I use these a lot with varying levels of success. The challenge is whether the listener recognizes your metaphor or just sees your hands flailing about. Thus, it is best to use these gestures with simple metaphors.
- Deictic gestures are gestures that may point to real objects or people, or those that exist in the world being described in your story. Again, instead of just saying a person was sitting across from you, point to where she was sitting so that we can be there with you.
- Beat gestures are small, short movements used to emphasize a point. An example would be pressing the forefinger and thumb together and thrusting them forward in the air in rhythm with each word you want to emphasize. Pausing at strategic times when telling your story is a common technique used to emphasize points or hold attention. The simplest application of a beat gesture can be used the same way, with the added benefit of controlling the eye.

You may use these gestures automatically, but many people prefer to tell instead of show because they do not want to look silly talking to people who aren't there, walking across the room to nowhere, or, more important, accidentally revealing a part of themselves they did not mean to. But being cautious doesn't make you a better storyteller. The more authentic the experience, the greater the connection the listener will feel with both the story and the storyteller. Strategically using the most powerful visual tool you own—yourself—is the most efficient way to do that.

Checklist for Using Body Language as a Tool

As you prepare to deliver your stories, ask yourself, are you:

✓ Aware of the nuances and idiosyncrasies of your body language?

✓ Willing to create intimacy through body language while telling your stories?

✓ Using expressions and gestures to convey emotion in a way that enhances the narrative?

Wrap-Up: What Does Your Body Say?

Body language is a powerful communication tool—so powerful that it can easily undermine what you say. It can also be used to enhance what you are saying by communicating what words cannot. Body language creates intimacy and trust, and helps you show emotion. Intimacy can be facilitated through eye contact and proximity. Expressions naturally convey emotion, but they only work as a facilitation tool if you are aware of how your expressions are influenced by your emotions. Gesturing can also reflect emotions, but again, they are only useful if you have insight into how you use them in your everyday communication. Consider how best to use these gestures as you facilitate with stories.

11

Storytellers Who Show and Tell

hen I was a child, my greatest fear was tornadoes. Actually, it is more accurate to say that I was afraid of tornado warnings. As a toddler, whenever the Emergency Broadcast System would run tests on television, I would hide under the dining room table, bracing for impact. Detroit had no instances of tornadoes during my childhood, but, although I stopped hiding under tables, I still had that fear as a 12-year-old going to summer band camp in Western Michigan. Tornadoes rarely touch down in major cities, but do you know where they do touch down? In Western Michigan.

One afternoon that summer, I got lost in the woods on the way back to my cabin in the pouring rain. As the storm siren blared and I watched storm clouds gather above, I remembered that we had been told to run to the lowest part of the camp in this situation, which on the girls' side was the beach. On the way to saving my life in the blinding rain, I ran into a clothesline neck first, with a force that knocked me out of my Velcro-fastened shoes, landing on my back in the mud. I got up, ran to the beach, and joined the other girls, who were huddling together and praying under blankets—all that protected us from a trip to Oz.

I don't know if a tornado actually formed that day. My preteen memory says that it did, but my adult brain believes that because no one was injured, a tornado was unlikely. The point is I lived and, as you can tell, I still remember every minute of that day. We all remember that pivotal moment when we have to face our greatest fear. It is even more memorable when your fear seeks you out. After that summer, I was no longer afraid of storm sirens, and while I still do not relish the thought of being in an actual tornado, I scratched them off my list of phobias.

You may be wondering why I am telling you my story about band camp. It is an example of a meaningful story with events and causal relationships that culminate with a change in the protagonist—that day I learned that I was brave, and could not be taken down by a clothesline I did not see coming (it later became a useful metaphor). Even while in the throes of my worst nightmare, I still could get up and keep running.

I also shared this story because it included actions you would feel compelled to perform. It is difficult to tell a story like that without looking up at the darkening sky, shivering to show how soaking wet you were, and, of course, running into a clothesline. This chapter is about purposefully and strategically acting out stories.

What It Means to Show

We have talked a lot about authenticity—about being real with yourself and the participants. It requires tapping into your oft-obscured inner life to fuel the outer life that people see. Life is easier if you are one of the lucky few whose inner and outer lives are the same: You think quirky thoughts and you do quirky things, you think funny things and you say funny things—because you are. Quirky and funny can be interesting to watch, but not everyone's "realness" is quirky and funny. If I'm being my real, true self, I would be at home, watching movies, while drinking tea. I prefer to let my mind dream up ideas and the strategies to implement them, or think about the big issues I am facing at the time. So to facilitate workshops or conduct meetings with subject matter experts, I need to find ways to take what I usually do in my head and do it out loud. What people see when I facilitate is a performance, one grounded in authenticity, but a performance nonetheless.

While my tendency to go inward has its disadvantages, there is one advantage that I treasure: I have a rich imagination, a vivid memory, and an ability to "see" and describe something that is not physically in front of me. If I am telling a story about an event that occurred, I go back there. I can tell you what happened just as I remember seeing it happen because I am no longer in the room with you.

What do you see when you tell a story? Where do you go? If you are telling a story about an ex-boss that micromanaged you and made you feel small, do you feel their presence hovering over you? Do you feel yourself recoil and shrink a little, just like you did back then? When you are describing a time you managed a successful project and your team commended you, do you smile, feeling the same pride you felt all those years ago when it happened? Or do you just remember the words without the nuanced layers of emotion or the sensory details?

Doug Stevenson's philosophy is based in the long-supported belief that showing is better than just telling. In his book *Story Theater Method: Strategic Storytelling in Business,* Stevenson (2008) writes, "The form of storytelling I believe works best in live performance is a combination of SHOW (act) and TELL (content). Instead of just narrating stories as past events, you will re-enact parts of them so they come alive." The feedback "show, don't tell" has followed me throughout my career. I first heard it when I started out as an instructional designer. The directive encouraged us to use examples and authentic exercises to teach a skill rather than simply telling the learner what to do. Naturally, storytelling was often the answer. Instructional designers would create scenarios that put learners at the center of the storm and make them use what they were learning to fight their way out.

Throughout my master's in writing program, instructors would routinely chastise us for writing something that was too "on the nose." If you have the opportunity to describe an event rather than telling the reader about it, take it. It is the difference between a character saying to her husband, "I am so angry with you" and instead having her ignore him as he follows her around the house, recoil from his touch at a dinner party, or seem fine when he is in the room, only to go into the bathroom and cry. She can do anything in your story besides actually telling the man she is mad.

In the facilitation industry, the "show, don't tell" philosophy looms large. Again, storytelling can save the day, but as you present your story, less telling and more showing leads to a greater impact. Before you get up in front of a group to facilitate, you have to shape and select your story, but that story is still nothing but a memory if you cannot bring it to life when you tell it. You must take the participants with you, and you can only do that if you can go back there yourself. Telling is a testimony; showing is a journey.

Like most of the strategies we have discussed in this book, I emphasize showing over telling because we want to tap into the listeners' emotions. I do not need a fancy metaphor for this—you know that you can feel what someone thinks of you based on their actions, before they tell you. Stories work the same way. I can tell you that I was freezing cold, running, and looking up at the storm clouds in the darkening sky, or, as I tell you, I could shiver, move my arms as I mimic running in place, and look up. I bet, with that same feeling of dread, you will look up with me.

Showing and Facilitating With Story

I know the word *performance* has a negative connotation when used to describe training, especially because we are supposed to be our authentic selves. Many see performance as putting on a show or pretending to be someone we are not. However, I do not agree. There are many aspects of your authentic self and each one manifests in its own way. And again, while your authentic self, is infinitely beautiful and fascinating to you, for the 20 people in the room watching you, shaping what they see is essential.

There is also another element at play here. You may be able to vividly remember what happened and have all the desire in the world to take listeners back there with you, but pulling that off takes skill beyond what they teach in your typical Training 101 course. You need to learn, at least at a high level, acting skills. Facilitators are trying to accomplish the same thing actors are, create the same experience, and have the same impact. Those who possess this skill naturally borrow several strategies from performers.

We ask a lot of our facilitators—and on top of everything else, you must also be a professional actor. It would be easy to give you a pass and say, "You don't have to be an actor, but . . . " or "You don't have to study acting, but . . . "; however, that is not my call. It is yours. Study as much or as little as you want; the bottom line is that the facilitators people will remember have a basic understanding of the actor's craft. Next, we will explore some of the strategies that actors and storytellers use to show instead of tell. We will look at the one-person show, bringing in substitutes for people who were part of the original story, and working with objects.

The One-Person Show

I have told my camp story a thousand times, highlighting different versions, meanings, or events, depending on the point I want to get across. I have longer versions where I mention that I lost my instrument or give vivid descriptions of the scary camp counselor in the cabin I stumbled upon in the dark. I have short versions where I focus on running into the unexpected clothesline. But every time I go back there, I can feel the brisk wind and rain lashing at my sleeveless arms. That sensory detail is essential to making the learners feel like they are there with you, but it also helps you remember how you felt, which is what the story is really about.

Remembering

If my story is already selected and shaped, then I remember the events and half the work is done. The other half happens when I tell the story, digging deeper to remember the sensory details—details that I use to show my story. My camp story is rich with detail that I can draw on to help me remember how I felt while it was happening. I may have time-lined the events , but remembering events is different from remembering the sensory details. I may not remember those until I am telling the story. I can timeline that I got lost, but I'll only feel how I felt when I talk about it—and see it.

The first thing I see is the dirt road outside the arts and crafts cabin. There is an eerie silence because there are no other kids around. (I assume their instructors let them out earlier due to the impending storm.) Remembering the silence makes me feel the same oppressive humidity I felt that day. I look up and the sky is getting darker, and with that detail comes my rising fear after realizing that I am lost.

So, to tap into how you felt during your experience, remember what you saw. Because there are often fears attached to what you saw or did not see, the feelings will accompany those details.

Performing the Show

As you remember the sensory details and begin acting them out, it may not seem very different from what happens when you are telling the story to one or two friends. But, whenever you are in front of a group, the only tool you have to bring the story to life is your body, so your movements need to get bigger and more pronounced. When using body language to enhance your stories, remember to act out instead of in. In other words, face the listeners or audience when you tell your story. Consider their point of view and what they would see if they were there with you.

In my camp story, I focus on the environment and my reaction to it. This is easier to act out because I know my own body and movements. But many stories include other people. If you are telling a story that includes a conversation you had or events that occurred with someone else, you need to consider ways to represent that other person, even though you are by yourself. The goal when acting out conversations is to avoid repeating "he said, she said" too often. The only way to include a different perspective is to use your own creativity to produce the other person.

One option is to alter your voice to distinguish the other person's voice from your own. The challenge with using this method is to ensure that your alternative voice does not sound mocking or condescending, unless, of course, that is your intent. When you do this, you'd simply face the participants as you act for yourself and the other person you're representing.

The other option is to literally have a conversation with yourself. First, establish a physical place for yourself, like facing left or right. Then, establish a space for the person you are talking to, typically across from you. Depending on who is talking, you will alternate between positions. You should still change your voice to distinguish who is talking, but because the listeners also have visual cues for who is talking, the distinction between voices won't need to be as strong.

Using a Supporting Cast

The challenge with physically alternating characters is that your movement can become distracting. One alternative to playing multiple roles yourself is to ask a participant to stand in for someone else. The ease with which you can get people to join in depends on a variety of factors, but there are a few things to keep in mind.

Casting and Recruiting

How you find the ideal person to include in your story depends on your philosophy about learners contributing to the experience. You could simply ask for volunteers, or take more of a "volun-tell" approach and ask a random person to come up and help. Let's look at examples of each:

- **Volunteer tips**
  - Knowing that you are going to ask for volunteers ahead of time helps. I start feeling out the group immediately and begin locking eyes and forming connections with people I think might volunteer if I asked. And then, when I do ask, I look directly at those people.
  - In your request for volunteers, tell them what you want them to do, instead of expecting them to be comfortable improvising with you. For example, say, "Can I have someone come up and help? I am going to play my ex-boss and you are going to play me."
- **Volun-tell tips**
  - Read the body language on display in the room. Some people would rather be hit by a truck than get up in front of the class and act out your story. If a person seems resistant, do not ask.
  - Speaking of people who seem resistant, I would discourage you from casting yourself as the "savior of shy people" and

bringing up someone who has been quiet the entire time, just to get them engaged. I have seen this happen a lot and it comes off as looking more about you than them.

o Make the activity you plan to engage them in short. People may be fine with doing something quick, but may not want to act out a four-hour telenovela with you.

Working With Others

"What I really want to do is direct." It used to be a running joke that all actors wanted to be directors. Well, as soon as you invite someone else into your scene, you are now an actor and a director, and it is not a responsibility you should take lightly. You are responsible for what happens when you invite others into the instructor's space. Remember, just because you are on a journey to authenticity and not afraid to look silly does not mean that your volunteer is, too. Do not make this person look ridiculous to entertain the rest of the group.

Here are a few tips for directing others:

- Do not assume your cast knows what you want. Explain what you want them to do and how you want it done either in private or in front of the class.
- Be careful with dialogue. No matter how many lines you give people, they may not remember them. It is best to let them say whatever you want them to say in their own words.
- Avoid highly emotional scenes with your cast. You may be putting someone in an awkward position, or cause the participant to have an unexpected reaction.

Working With Objects

Object work is a term used by improvisers to describe working with objects that are not visible. There are a few objects in my camp story, but the clothesline stands out the most, for obvious reasons. When I told you I ran into a clothesline, did you picture what that would look like? Did you picture a 12-year-old girl becoming air-bound for a few seconds, or just falling flat on her back? Maybe I bounced off the clothesline, stepped back a few paces, and then slipped on the mud. In many cases, it does not matter, but in other cases how something happened is important. The content is static, but how you tell the story influences what the listener sees. Remember, the story of me running into the clothesline will become the listener's story of me telling them how I ran into a clothesline. Being able to paint the picture for them helps.

Here are a few tips for using object work in your stories:

- Practice by handling the items you frequently encounter and be aware of how you work with them. How do you position your hands when you hold a mug? How does that differ from when you are drinking from the mug?
- Always complete an action. Once you are finished drinking your coffee, the mug should not vanish into thin air—put it down on the conveniently nearby invisible desk.
- Exaggerate your hand movements while working with the objects to emphasize their shape and how they function. Also, go slow. Do not drink your imaginary coffee as fast as you drink real coffee!

Checklist for Showing and Telling

As you prepare to deliver your stories, ask yourself, are you:

✓ Able and willing to physically portray elements of your story, rather than just describing them?

✓ Able to vocally or physically represent the other people who played a role in your original story?

✓ Willing to ask participants to portray supporting parts as you tell your story? Do you know how to support them?

Wrap-Up: Showtime!

Storytelling is a performance that is rooted in authenticity. It comes more naturally to some than others, but what matters is possessing the ability to tap into other aspects of your personality that will help you portray the story so participants feel like they are there with you.

Make sure you are facing the audience as much as possible when you perform, regardless of how the events played out when they happened. If other people were present, try to either represent them yourself by altering your voice and physical position, or recruiting a supporting cast to help you. Also, when working with imaginary objects, make exaggerated, yet realistic hand movements and ensure that you finish each movement (for example, put the plate that you picked up back down on the table).

12

The Facilitating With Story Process

The previous chapters focused on the "whys" and "hows" of facilitating with story, but when you are staring at a calendar packed with upcoming facilitation engagements, it is perhaps more helpful to focus primarily on the "hows." This chapter serves as both a recap and a tool to use as you prepare to use stories to facilitate your next learning experience.

All the topics we have discussed so far are dependent on one another, and together they make the facilitating with story process (Figure 12-1).

Figure 12-1. Facilitating With Story Process

Step 1: Identify a Story That Will Support a Point

Start building your cache of stories—both old and new. Chapter 1 provided four sources of existing, untapped stories: your professional career, the people in your life, the events in your life, and your values. First, live for the story—take risks, ask questions, do the unexpected. But, you must also be observant and, most of all, reflective. Be willing to look back and make sense of what happened. Save and shape what is usable and have it ready when you need it, which means that you already know the point the story broadly supports. And remember, if you need a story, follow the truth.

When you are considering a story, you must determine whether it has qualities that facilitate effective learning. We looked at each element in chapters 4 through 7.

Stories That Connect

The primary reason to tell a story while facilitating is to clarify points and create meaning, as we discussed in chapter 4. Stories do this by revealing connections among content, experiences, and people.

Remember, the story should:

- Reveal connections between the content and real-life experience.
- Help learners link existing ideas to new ones.
- Encourage learners to connect their own experiences and ultimately see the world from a different point of view.

Stories That Show Change

Writers and storytellers will tell you that all effective stories show a change in people or circumstances. However, change is one of the most difficult aspects to tackle because it requires honesty, introspection, and time to reflect and identify a change that is real.

In chapter 5, we determined that your story should:

- Provide examples of positive outcomes so learners are motivated to make the change.
- Help ensure learners understand that making the change is within their power.
- Give guidance on how to make the change.

Stories That Are Relevant

I wish that it could go without saying that a story should be relevant to the listener. Unfortunately, as I mentioned in chapter 6, I have seen too many facilitators miss the mark with stories that are either too narrow or too broad.

Remember, your story should:

- Have a clear, core message that speaks to a universal truth.
- Speak to an emotional experience that is common to most people.
- Encourage learners to tell their own stories.

Stories That Entertain

You should always strive to tell stories that create a pleasurable experience instead of just dropping a flat narrative into someone's lap. As discussed in chapter 7, while "entertaining" does not always require making people laugh, a little funny goes a long way. We are also entertained by surprise or anything unexpected.

Remember, your story should:

- Incorporate elements of suspense.
- Contain surprises or otherwise be amusing.

Step 2: Identify the Focal Point of the Story

The point that the story supports is different from the point of the story. Several stories can support one broad point, and one story can support several broad points. This step focuses on identifying the point of the story itself—the meaning of the story.

Step 3: Timeline the Story's Events

We use timelining to identify the key event that carries the story, as well as the leading events that immediately precede the key event and the consequential events that followed. Timelining is covered in chapter 1.

Step 4: Structure and Shape the Story

Once you have identified a reason to tell your story, found a story that supports an idea you are facilitating, and determined the point of the story itself, you are ready to structure and shape your story.

Chapter 3 explores the types of structuring models. Recipe models focus on what elements to include in the story you are structuring. The hero's journey, like similar recipe models, provides both plot points and the order in which those points should go. It also helps you identify the meaning of the story, because it encourages you to identify the what, how, and why of the protagonist's transformation.

We also used the story spine framework to explore building blocks structures. Building blocks models are more focused on the elements that should be included in the story, not the specific type of content. In this method, you are only building on events and the connections between them.

The module I use is a variation of the building blocks structure, and includes intent, context, action, and point (ICAP). This method provides structure without being rigid, and it takes a further step back to consider the larger picture. Here's a review of the model:

- **Intent:** What Do I Want the Story to Do?
  - First decide what you want the story to do. The intent influences the entire story.
- **Context:** Where Am I Taking Them?
  - This is where you consider the intent of your story, and where you plan to take your listeners while on the journey.
- **Action:** What Are the Leading, Key, and Consequential Events?
  - Every compelling story needs action to move it forward. The ICAP model takes advantage of the timelining strategy to identify the leading, key, and consequential events. It recognizes the key story structure in the relationship, and the dependencies among the events that make up the story.
- **Point:** How Will Learners Gain From This Story?
  - Finally, you must identify strategies to facilitate learners through the "point construction" process. Remember, the intent is your goal, but the point belongs to the learner. It is the difference between telling learners what the point is, and having a discussion that helps the learners identify the point

for themselves. Just make sure you consider how to do this before delivering the course—it should be part of your story structuring process.

Step 5: Facilitate the Story

All the work that goes into selecting and shaping stories goes out the window if the story is not delivered well. Chapters 8 through 11 focused on the storyteller and how to facilitate with story, exploring four considerations for creating an effective learning experience: revealing yourself, inviting listeners in, using body language, and showing and telling.

Storytellers Reveal Themselves

The privilege of facilitating learning asks much of the trainer. As we discussed in chapter 8, the front of the room is the most powerful place to be, and it is a position that needs to be earned over and over again. An effective way to harness that power and use it as a tool is to give it all away. And the best way to do that is to create an environment where people feel empowered to be themselves and allow themselves to make mistakes. What better model for that than a leader who is authentic, vulnerable, and present?

As you tell your story:

- Facilitate with authenticity as your primary goal.
- Create and support an environment where you and your participants feel comfortable being vulnerable.
- Trust yourself, your participants, and the relationship you are building through this experience.

Storytellers Invite Listeners In

You may have noticed that when talking about facilitating with story, I frequently mentioned giving stuff away. It is a reminder that your experience should not be your focus. The focus should be on the learners and how they are experiencing the story you crafted for them. It is your responsibility to include learners in the process by inviting them in.

In chapter 9, we discussed the importance of inviting learners in:

- Let go of your stories because your stories are transformed from the story of your experience into their story of hearing you talk about that experience.
- Ask for contribution by asking open-ended questions about how the experience you are describing relates to the learners' experiences. Facilitate this process—do not expect learners to volunteer information on their own.
- Be quiet and do not answer your own questions. Wait and be comfortable sitting in the silence.

Storytellers Use Body Language as a Tool

In chapter 10, I described how your body is communicating whether you want it to or not. If you do not approach this form of communication with intent, how you move—or don't move—may tell a different story from the one that is coming out of your mouth. Make sure to:

- Be aware of the nuances and idiosyncrasies of your body language.
- Create intimacy through body language while telling your stories.
- Use expressions and gestures to convey emotion in a way that enhances the narrative.

Storytellers Show and Tell

Take your listeners with you. It is always better to act out your stories than to simply tell them. It not only makes the story more engaging, but also helps create connections and deepen the listener's understanding of what you are attempting to convey.

You may decide to do a one-person show or invite (or recruit) others to join you. If you tackle this by yourself, you'll have to find a way to distinguish the characters from one another. If you are joined by others, you'll have to direct the scene. Do not assume that participants will understand what you want them to do. When you show your story, you can:

- Physically portray elements of your story rather than just describe them.
- Vocally or physically represent the other people who played a role in your original story.

- Ask participants to portray supporting parts as you tell your story and support them throughout the process.

"Tell the Truth as You Understand It."

If something inside of you is real, we will probably find it interesting, and it will probably be universal. So you must risk placing real emotion at the center of your work. Write straight into the emotional center of things. Write toward vulnerability. Don't worry about appearing sentimental. Worry about being unavailable; worry about being absent or fraudulent. Risk being unliked. Tell the truth as you understand it.

— Anne Lamott, *Bird by Bird: Some Instructions on Writing and Life*

Anne Lamott's book *Bird by Bird* (1994) was a revelation. The first time I read it, I was studying nonfiction writing. It was a time of constant remembering, reliving, and revealing the stories that made up my life—only to question their accuracy and the relevance of the lessons I learned from them. It was the cost of separating the writing life I was creating for myself from my life as a consultant.

Then, as I prepared to write this book, I reread *Bird by Bird* for inspiration. Far removed from graduate school, I viewed it through the lens of a facilitator who uses storytelling as a strategy. Many of the lessons in it applied to both creative nonfiction writing and corporate storytelling. It seems obvious now—stories are stories. They come from the same source: my life. They reflect who I was, who I am, and who I will become. And they have value—but only if I am willing to look at them, pull them apart, and make them useful. Lamott's advice to not worry about telling the truth or being vulnerable, and instead worry about being absent or fraudulent, became the driving force behind how I find, shape, and tell my stories.

I will never know whether you will walk away from this book with the motivation to find the narratives that shape your life and use them as tools to teach others. But I hope you do. Remember, my stories stopped being completely mine once I shared them with you. You will take them in and interpret them in a way that is most useful for you. The same will happen to your stories once you use them to help participants make connections. All you can do now is make more stories for the storyteller who lives inside you—inside all of us.

So, live more, learn more, and share more. One story at a time.

Acknowledgments

First, thank you to the many clients, subject matter experts, and class participants who've shared their stories with me and listened to mine through the years. All your voices mattered and I've never taken that for granted.

To Gary Hernandez, who encouraged me to stop dreaming and start doing.

To Ana Maria Barella, who pushed me to value my voice.

To Stephanie Riddle, my cousin, friend, and cheerleader.

To Amanda Smith, for giving me the feedback to improve my proposal and then championing the idea through the process.

To my editors, Kathryn Stafford and Melissa Jones, for their expertise and patience.

To Karin Rex, Jim Smith Jr., and Jonathan Halls for sharing their storytelling philosophies and strategies with me.

To everyone who told me I should write a book one day—I did. And I hope whatever you saw in me shines through these pages.

References

Abela, A. 2013. *Advanced Presentations By Design: Creating Communication That Drives Action.* San Francisco: John Wiley & Sons.

Ambrose, S.A., M.W. Bridges, M.C. Lovett, M. DiPietro, and M.K. Norman. 2010. *How Learning Works: Seven Research-Based Principles for Smart Teaching.* San Francisco: Jossey-Bass.

Beard, A. 2014. "Leading With Humor." *Harvard Business Review.* https://hbr.org/2014/05/leading-with-humor.

Brown, B. 2010. *The Gifts of Imperfection: Let Go of Who You Think You're Supposed to Be and Embrace Who You Are.* Center City, MN: Hazelden Publishing.

Campbell, J. 2008. *The Hero With A Thousand Faces.* Novato, CA: New World Library.

Chan, J. 2010. *Training Fundamentals: Pfeiffer Essential Guides to Training Basics.* San Francisco: John Wiley & Sons.

Cleland, J. 2016. *Mastering Suspense, Structure, and Plot: How to Write Gripping Stories That Keep Readers on the Edge of Their Seats.* Blue Ash, OH: Writer's Digest Books.

Cron, L. 2012. *Wired For Story: The Writer's Guide to Using Brain Science to Hook Readers From the Very First Sentence.* New York: Ten Speed Press.

Dale Carnegie Training. 2011. *Stand and Deliver: How to Become a Masterful Communicator and Public Speaker.* New York: Simon & Schuster.

Dolan, G. 2017. *Stories for Work: The Essential Guide to Business Storytelling.* Milton Qld, Australia: John Wiley & Sons.

Greengross, G., and G.F. Miller. 2008. "Dissing Oneself Versus Dissing Rivals: Effects of Status, Personality, and Sex on the Short-Term and Long-Term Attractiveness of Self-Deprecating and Other-Deprecating Humor." *Evolutionary Psychology,* July 1.

Jackson, W. 2011. *Stories At Work.* Aukland, New Zealand: Pindar NZ.

Keith-Spiegel, P. 1964. "Early Conception of Humor: Varieties and Issues." Chapter 1 in *The Psychology of Humor: Theoretical Perspectives and Empirical Issues,* edited by J.H. Goldstein and P.E. McGhee, Chicago: University of Chicago Press.

Knowles, M.S., E.F. Holton, and R.A. Swanson. 2005. *The Adult Learner: The Definitive Classic in Adult Education and Human Resource Development,* 6th ed. Burlington, MA: Elsevier.

Lamott, A. 1994. *Bird by Bird: Some Instructions on Writing and Life.* New York: Anchor Books.

Leitman, M. 2015. *Long Story Short: The Only Storytelling Guide You'll Ever Need.* Seattle: Sasquatch Books.

Library of Congress. n.d. "The North Wind & the Sun." Adapted from *The Aesop for Children: With Pictures by Milo Winter,* Chicago: Rand, McNally & Co (1919). http://read.gov/aesop/143.html.

Lipman, D. 1999. *Improving Your Storytelling: Beyond the Basics for All Who Tell Stories in Work and Play.* Little Rock, AR: August House.

Navarro, J. 2008. *What Every BODY Is Saying: An Ex-FBI Agent's Guide to Speed-Reading People.* New York: HarperCollins.

Pink, D.H. 2012. *To Sell Is Human: The Surprising Truth About Moving Others.* New York: Riverhead.

Provine, R.R. 2001. *Laughter: A Scientific Investigation.* New York: Penguin.

Shatz, M., and M. Helitzer. 2016. *Comedy Writing Secrets: The Best-Selling Guide to Writing Funny and Getting Paid for It.* Blue Ash, OH: Writer's Digest Books.

Snyder, B. 2005. *Save The Cat! The Last Book on Screenwriting You'll Ever Need.* Studio City, CA: Michael Wiese Productions.

Stevenson, D. 2008. *Doug Stevenson's Story Theater Method: Strategic Storytelling in Business.* Colorado Springs: Cornelia Press.

Uono, S., and J.K. Hietanen. 2015. "Eye Contact Perception in the West and East: A Cross-Cultural Study." *PLoS ONE,* February 25.

About the Author

Hadiya Nuriddin is the owner for Focus Learning Solutions, a learning design and development provider for both corporate and academic organizations. Hadiya has decades of experience in designing, developing, and delivering both technical and professional development courses and she specializes in creating effective, engaging, and interactive online learning solutions. When she is not working with clients, she consults with other self-employed L&D professionals to help them start and build their own businesses. She has a master's degree in both education (MEd) and writing and publishing (MA). She is also a Certified Professional in Learning and Performance (CPLP).

Index

In this index, *f* denotes figure.